Memory Drawing:
Perceptual Training and Recall

Memory Drawing
Perceptual Training and Recall

Darren R. Rousar

Velatura Press LLC, Publisher   Minneapolis, Minnesota USA

Memory Drawing: *Perceptual Training and Recall*
by Darren R. Rousar

First published in 2013 by **Velatura Press LLC**
www.velaturapress.com | www.memorydrawing.com | www.studiorousar.com

ISBN-13: 978-0-9800454-4-4
ISBN-10: 0-9800454-4-4
First Printing, 2013
Printed in the United States of America

Library of Congress Cataloging-in-Publication Data
Rousar, Darren R.
  Memory Drawing: Perceptual Training for the Representational Artist / by Darren R. Rousar.
  Includes index.
  ISBN-13: 978-0-9800454-4-4
  ART028000   ART / Techniques / General
  ART052000   ART / Techniques / Life Drawing
  ART010000   ART / Techniques / Drawing

Library of Congress Control Number: 2013932243

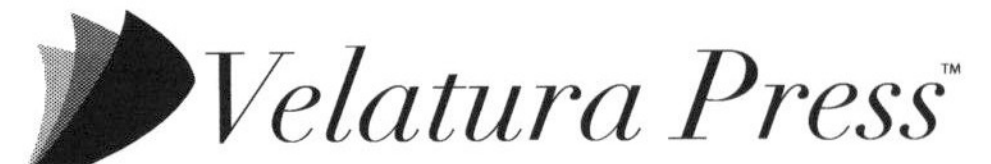
Velatura Press™ Minneapolis, Minnesota USA

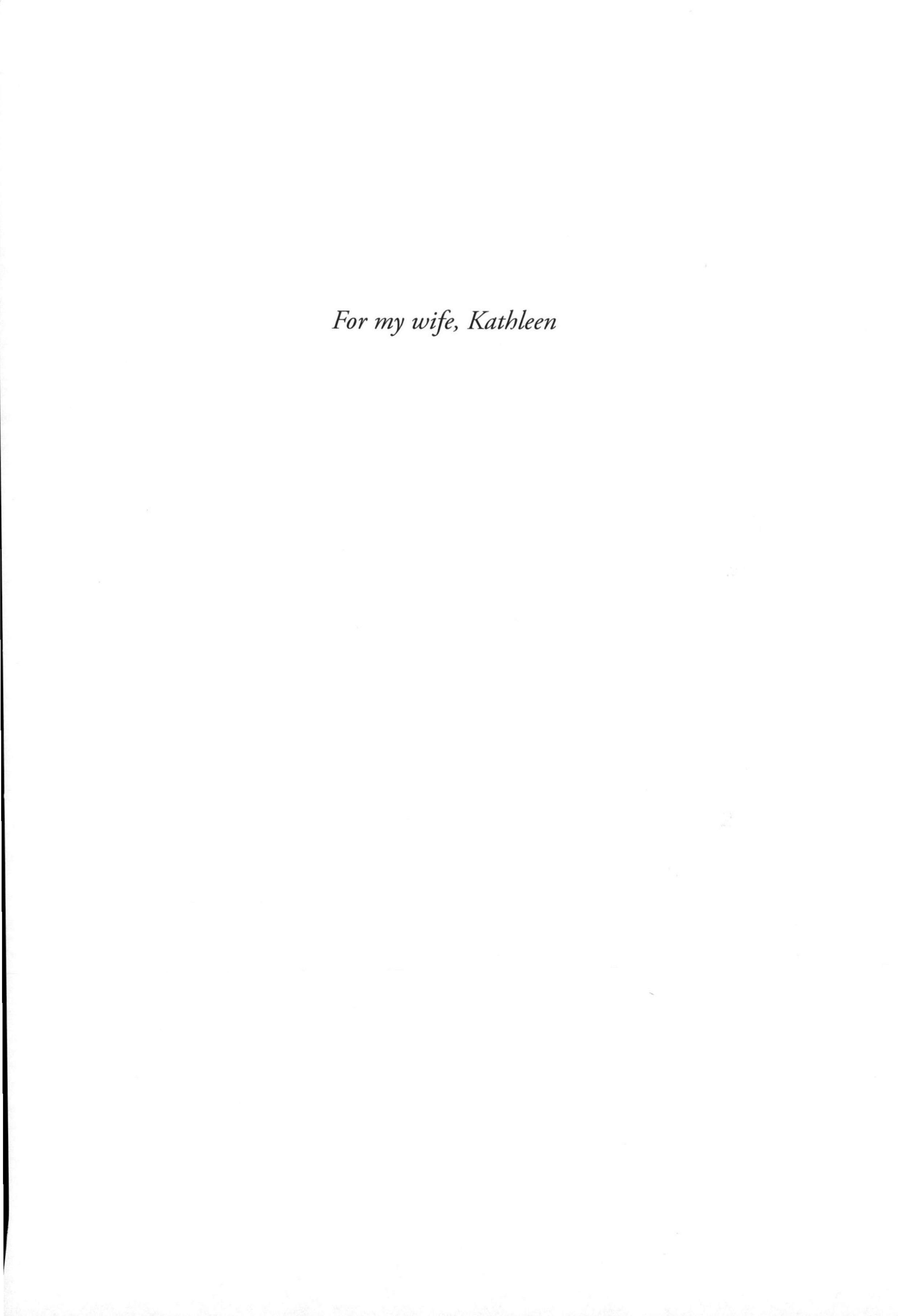

For my wife, Kathleen

Thank you, Linda Crank.
You are a gentle and patient editor in addition to being a wonderful artist.
This book would not be what it is had it not been for your input.
http://lacrank.com

Thank you as well to the other eyes on this project:
Kirk Richards - http://www.kirkrichards.com
Matthew J. Collins - http://matthewjamescollins.com

·Table of Contents·

Introduction   9

History   15

Science   33

Process   41

Shape   45

Value   71

Color   91

Advanced Memory Drawing   99

Sculptural Memory   105

Appendix I   Sage Advice from Père Lecoq   111

Appendix II Harold Speed: The Visual Memory   115

Appendix III Curves or Facets?   121

Appendix IV Copying Old Master Drawings   125

Glossary   129

Index   133

·Introduction·

I have discovered that it is of some use when you lie in bed at night and gaze into the darkness to repeat in your mind the things you have been studying. Not only does it help the understanding, but also the memory.   -Leonardo da Vinci

At the outset the reader should note that throughout this book I will use the term *memory drawing* to mean both memory drawing as well as memory painting. For those so inclined, this would also include sculpture (see the chapter on sculptural memory).

Why should an artist bother to train their visual memory, and what does that even mean? Can't I just paint what's in front of me, or from a photograph, or from my imagination? These are the kinds of questions I get from students when I bring up the subject of memory drawing. This book answers these questions and provides a curriculum for training your abilities to perceive as well as to remember.

Lest We Forget

Clearly an artist's ability to recall something previously seen gives that artist a distinct advantage. That advantage is all the more when the artist's subject is no longer in view. If you think about it, all life drawing and painting is at some point being done from the artist's memory, even if that memory is only a few seconds old. Every time the artist takes their eyes off of the model or scene and looks at their paper or canvas, their visual memory is involved. What if that artist's visual memory was highly trained? That artist might need the model for a shorter period of time, or might have a more productive time when the model is in pose. He or she might be better at painting all of the fleeting effects that nature throws at one when we are landscape painting *en plein air*.

See and Perceive

In Arthur Conan Doyle's short story, *A Scandal in Bohemia*, Sherlock Holmes comments to Watson that he sees but he does not observe. This is in reference to Watson's bafflement at Holmes' deductive abilities.

> *"You see, but you do not observe. The distinction is clear. For example, you have frequently seen the steps which lead up from the hall to this room."*

"Frequently."

"How often?"

"Well, some hundreds of times."

"Then how many are there?"

"How many? I don't know."

"Quite so! You have not observed. And yet you have seen. That is just my point. Now, I know that there are seventeen steps, because I have both seen and observed."[1]

Whether the goal is drawing, painting or sculpting, memory drawing begins with an intentional effort to visually observe the subject. How well the subject is remembered is directly related to how well it is observed. In other words, artists need to become expert observers in order to have exceptional visual memories. This is true for many fields and very often the memory skill of experts is geared towards their expertise.[2] In a sense, they expect to see what they are trained to see. They look for it.

As the subtitle states, this book is as much about learning to perceive what you see as it is about memory drawing.*

The Right Sort of Education

Memory-drawing training for art students reached its peak during the late nineteenth to early twentieth century. However, even back then its prominence in arts education had begun to wane. Kenyon Cox (1856-1919), an American art student of Carolus-Duran and Gérôme, who was also an influential arts commentator, had this to say about the state of memory drawing in his day:

> *I think in almost all modern training in art there is a lamentable neglect of the training of the memory. I have frequently been astonished to find that artists of great ability have apparently no visual memory and are unable to do anything without the immediate presence of the model. This seems to me to be a patent evidence of a lack of the right sort of education. . . I should feel that half the value of a sound training in drawing was lost if it were not made to include a training of the memory as well as of the eye and hand.*[3]

The prevalence of photography and the rise of non-representational art seems to have nullified the usefulness of training one's visual memory just as the practice was beginning to be formalized. However, as useful as photographic reference is for some artists, in many respects it is a pale substitute for a trained visual memory.

---

*Cognitive psychologists (those who study perception, memory and the brain) tend to prefer the terms *perceive* and *perception* over observe and observation. Since they are synonymous, for the most part I will do the same.

R. H. Ives Gammell and Richard F. Lack

R. H. Ives Gammell was arguably one of the last, direct links between French nineteenth-century picture-making and today.[4] He taught many American art students and a number of them went onto teach others. Some, like Charles Cecil, Thomas Dunlay, Paul Ingbretson and Carl Samson are still teaching today. Part of Gammell's instruction included memory drawing, and he recommended that his students read a book about the subject called, *The Training of the Memory in Art,*[5] by a French teacher named Horace Lecoq de Boisbaudran.

Richard F. Lack,[6] a Gammell student who was also one of my teachers, somewhat systematized memory training for his own atelier students. As Gammell had done before him, Lack based his procedures on Boisbaudran's book. He also wrote a brief article about this subject in a privately-published journal, the *Classical Realism Quarterly.*[7]

Just how strongly Lack believed in memory drawing can be seen in the following quote from that article:

> *Memory must be integrated into a mature painter's working method if his or her talent is to be truly fulfilled. I myself, when doing a portrait commission, will spend up to three times as much time on memory work as I do on direct observation.*[8]

In varying degrees, Boisbaudran, Gammell and Lack (as well as my principle teachers, Annette LeSueur and Charles H. Cecil) informed my own memory training and as such this book is an extension of their teachings.

A Daunting Task

Although I encourage you to consistently engage in memory-drawing practice, it should not supplant your regular art exercises. Memory-drawing ought to be done in addition to your regular art training, not instead of it. In a perfect world it would be integrated into traditional arts instruction, but the reality is that you will most likely be training your visual memory on your own.

You should be aware that what I present in these pages is an extensive and intense course. Achieving your best level will take a consistent, concerted effort over a long period of time, just like what is needed when learning to play an instrument, speak a foreign language or learning to draw, paint or sculpt.

Without a teacher to guide and encourage you along the way your motivation is entirely up to you. Do you need to do every exercise in the book? Perhaps, and more. Your visual memory is like a muscle, it needs maintenance to stay strong, and it is no coincidence that the exercises in this book are called just that, *exercises.* Once you get a sense of what memory drawing is all about and you gain some proficiency in it, you will be better able to determine how much, how often and exactly what exercises to do in order to improve and maintain your visual memory. If you can commit to doing all of the exercises in this book, you will see a marked improvement over time.

But let me backtrack on that a little bit. More important than doing each and every exercise is simply doing some exercises on a regular basis. Once you become more adept at visual perception, memory training can evolve into something less formal. Again, do not let your regular art training suffer, rather, try to incorporate memory training into it. When the trajectory of your regular art training takes you into creating your own artworks, your memory-drawing efforts will also likely be incorporated into those creations. As such, memory-drawing may cease being structured exercises and become a part of the process.

Keep your eye on the prize: a well-developed visual memory that will be an ever present aid as you produce whatever artworks you set out to create.

Chapter Summaries

Chapter 1 - History

The history of memory drawing is long, but unfortunately not very well known. This chapter will help to inform you of its past. Hopefully, history will not repeat itself, and memory drawing will once again be an important part of an art student's training.

Chapter 2 - Science

As you might imagine, the research about memory is extensive. Many books and hundreds of academic papers have been written on the subject. Distilling these into the aspects which deal with our visual memory is the main task dealt with in this chapter. The summary background provided in the chapter should help the student understand how their mind perceives and remembers visual information.

Chapter 3 - Process

To get from one place to another you must follow a set of directions. These can be as simple as being pointed to the destination or as complicated as making *pâté en croûte.*[9] Knowing what informs the directions can often be helpful because it gives the person the ability to put the directions to their best use. These principles are outlined in the chapter on process.

Chapter 4 - Shape

Perception and memory-drawing begins with shape. This chapter takes the student from simple line comparison all the way through complex figure drawings.

Chapter 5 - Value

Our perception of values is different than for shape. Therefore, the process of memorizing value observations is different as well. The chapter on value begins with learning how to perceive pairs of flat tones. The student then progresses to simple images in full value, to observing and recalling actual, real-world scenes, and finally, reproducing Old Master paintings from memory.

Chapter 6 - Color

Color is a complex topic, especially given all of the different variables involved. This chapter attempts to simplify the issue and gives the student guidance on how color perception and color memory can best be trained.

Chapter 7 - Advanced Memory Drawing

Advanced memory-drawing is that which is done from the direct observation of nature. This chapter advises the advanced student on the best ways to practice their visual memory skills when landscape painting and for other fleeting observations.

Chapter 8 -Sculptural Memory Drawing

The basis for sculpting from one's memory is similar to many of the principles in the preceding chapters. This chapter goes further and provides the student of sculpture with exercises in three-dimensions.

Appendix I - Sage Advice from Père Lecoq

This appendix is a reprint of the first appendix in Boisbaudran's book, *The Training of the Memory in Art*. In it, Boisbaudran summarizes his teachings on memory training.

Appendix II - Harold Speed: The Visual Memory

The classic book on drawing is *The Practice and Science of Drawing* - by Harold Speed. It was originally published in 1913 and since then has impacted many students. In his book, Speed wrote a chapter which explained his thoughts on an artist's visual memory. This appendix is a reprint of that chapter.

Appendix III - Facets or Curves?

There are many ways to begin a drawing, whether from life or from memory, and two of them are faceting and curving. This appendix discusses historical reasons for pursuing both approaches.

Appendix IV - Copying Old Master Drawings

One of the ways students learn sound drawing technique is through copying Old Master drawings. This appendix outlines the process, based upon Gammell's assertion that the student's copies of Old Master drawings should be exact.

Onward

Certain aspects of this book could continue, almost endlessly, but every author faces a deadline. Fortunately we have the internet! Updates to this book, further exercises and more are available at www.memorydrawing.com and www.studiorousar.com.

1 Doyle, Arthur Conan. "Adventures of Sherlock Holmes - Adventure 1: A Scandal in Bohemia." *The Strand Magazine*, July 1891, 61-77.
2 Magnussen, Svein and Helstrup, Tore. *Everyday Memory*. New York: Psychology Press, 2007.
3 Cox, Kenyon. *Art Museums and Schools: Four Lectures Delivered at the Metropolitan Museum of Art*. New York: C. Scribner's Sons, 1913. Pages 62-64.
4 Gammell, R. H. Ives. *Twilight of Painting*. New York: G.P. Putnam's Sons, 1946. *Twilight of Painting*, is a must-read for anyone interested in representational art. Also see, Ackerman, Gerald M., and Elizabeth Ives Hunter. *Transcending Vision: R. H. Ives Gammell, 1893-1981*. R.H. Ives Gammell Studios Trust, 2001.
5 Boisbaudran, Horace Lecoq de. *The Training of the Memory in Art and the Education of the Artist*. London: Macmillan and Co. Limited, 1914. See: http://archive.org/details/TheTrainingOfTheMemoryInArtAndTheEducationOfTheArtist
6 Gjertson, Stephen. *Richard F. Lack, An American Master*. Minneapolis: The American Society of Classical Realism, 2001. As an aside, Richard Lack initially coined the term "Classical Realism" in 1982 for an exhibition catalog, *Classical Realism, The Other Twentieth Century*. For more on its history, see Gjertson, Stephen. "Classical Realism: A Living Artistic Tradition." *Stephen Gjertson Galleries*. N.p., 11 2010. Web. 12 April 2012. <http://stephengjertsongalleries.com/?p=505>.
7 Lack, Richard F. "Memory Training For Painters." *Classical Realism Quarterly*. V.2 (1990): 18-21. This article is available through my website, here: http://www.studiorousar.com/2013/01/08/richard-lack-on-memory-drawing/
8 *Ibid.*, page 21.
9 Culinary Institute of America. "How to Make Pâté en Croûte." http://chefsblade.monster.com. http://chefsblade.monster.com/training/articles/712-how-to-make-pt-en-crote (accessed January 22, 2013).

·History·

I will tell you my idea of a portrait, said Corot: Let a person walk slowly through an open door, about ten feet away from you; let him pass and repass a few times; then if, after he has gone, you can paint the image which he has left in your brain, you will paint a portrait. If you sit down before him, you begin to count his buttons.[1]

Through the years artists have sought to improve their visual memory for four distinct and yet not always exclusive reasons:

- to develop the ability to accurately recall something which they had previously seen
- to remember fleeting effects
- to recall the essentials of something which they had previously seen
- to enhance their imagination

Behind these distinctions are factors which, in part, motivated representational artists as well as representational arts education. Because of this, it is helpful to look at those factors in some detail because they can impact how memory-drawing training is undertaken.

An Artist's Outward Vision

Broadly speaking, those artists on one side of the representational coin were those for whom recreating what they observed was the highest form of artistic achievement and joy. Part of their training was learning to artfully adjust what was seen, only after a certain level of accuracy was attained. The late nineteenth-century English artist Walter Crane, a student of Ruskin and the author of the book *Line & Color*, called this kind of motivation for painting an example of the "outward vision."[2] He also defines this quite well, but it is important to remember when reading his definition that he is writing about an accomplished artist, not a student in training.

> *The painter and the sculptor often seek as complete a representation as possible, and what may be called complete representation is within the range of their resources. Yet unless some individual choice or feeling impresses the work of either kind it is not a re-presentation [sic], but becomes an imitation, and therefore inartistic.*[3]

An Artist's Inward Vision

The other main group of representational artists were those who pursued more of an internal source for what they put on their canvases. Crane called this the "inward vision," claiming that:

> [It] *is not bound by the appearances of the particular moment. It is the record of the sum of many moments, and retains the typical impress of multitudinous and successive impressions. . . [It] re-creates rather than represents, and its virtue consists in the vividness and beauty with which, in the language of line, form, and color, these visions of the mind are recorded and presented to the outward eye.*[4]

Of course there are any number of philosophies in-between and inasmuch as the divisions existed (and in many ways they still do), they also affected which goals of memory drawing were emphasized. What is immensely important however is that most of the books and writings which mention memory training state that the accuracy of one's memory, much like Crane's outward vision, was to be pursued. Once trained, one's inward vision could then be realized more effectively on paper, canvas or in stone.[5]

Memory's Role in Imagination, Invention and Selection

Memory and one's imagination are believed by many to be linked. Undergoing less of a debate is the idea that one's visual memory is subconsciously selective. Many artists claimed to have made use of the fact that the accuracy of one's visual recall is often limited to summary information and that our imagination completes the image. Left on its own, our mind seems to choose what it wants to remember from what is visually perceived. These kinds of memories were considered by some artists to be focused, essential facts. They were used as filtered perceptions from which to gain inspiration and thereby enhance their imagination.

In his second discourse, given before the Royal Academy in 1769, Sir Joshua Reynolds spoke of the inventive power of our memory:

> *Invention, strictly speaking, is little more than a new combination of those images which have been previously gathered and deposited in the memory: nothing can come of nothing.*[6]

As true as this may be, the stored images Reynolds was speaking about were based more on a serious study of the Old Masters as well as the sculpture of classical antiquity, than the things one routinely saw in everyday life. In this sense, memory was used to recall the ideal of past masters.

Memory was also seen as a selective filter during the late nineteenth and early twentieth-centuries. Beyond selectivity, which was sought for as a means to instill the "ideal" in one's artwork, many artists of these time periods believed that memory was a means to further connect with the viewer. The theory was that when painting from memory, the artist recalled what was seen in a way that was a step removed from the source. This removal allowed the artist to paint less of a literal copy of the scene than a recollection of the essential characteristics, feelings, and impressions which moved the artist in the first place. The artist's intent was that when looking at the painting, the viewer would bring forth their own memories of similar scenes. This allowed the viewer to project their own memories into the painting, and complete the painting themselves in their mind's eye. Supposedly, the viewer could then better experience the emotive aspects of the piece.

The American landscape painter George Inness was an ardent proponent of painting from one's memory due to the selective, emotional aspects associated with it. He believed that the artist's primary task was to motivate the viewer's mind to feel while looking at the painting.

> [The artist's task is] *simply to reproduce in other minds the impression which a scene has made upon him . . . A work of art does not appeal to the intellect. It does not appeal to the moral sense. Its aim is not to instruct, not to edify, but to awaken an emotion . . . Details in the picture must be elaborated only enough* [to] *fully reproduce the impression that the artist wishes to reproduce. When more than this is done, the impression is weakened or lost, and we see simply an array of external things which may be very cleverly painted, and may look very real, but which do not make an artistic painting.*[7]

Inness' son, an artist himself, claimed that his father rarely painted directly from nature but would observe and draw a scene from the same spot, day after day. Then, when back in the studio and in a fit of inspiration, he would create a painting from those memories, oftentimes ignoring the studies he had made while on location.[8]

William Morris Hunt, an American student of Couture and later influenced by Millet, became an influential teacher himself in mid-nineteenth-century Boston. One of his students kept notes of his teachings, and these were later put into book form around the time of Hunt's death. Hunt was as interested in memory drawing as Inness, and the subject occurs over and over again in his *Art Talks*.[9] In one of his many notes, Hunt says that he believed the best landscape paintings were painted from memory, but only after serious study when in front of nature. This was because, in his opinion, when painting directly from nature the artist was so intent on representing what was being seen that the compositional aspects of picture-making were forgotten.[10]

The American landscape painter, Bruce Crane fleshed out this concept even more.

> *The object of studying and sketching out of doors is to fill the memory with facts. It should therefore be exact and conscientious. But in the studio the artist should use his knowledge freely. Nature seldom presents pictures ready-made, and the best effects last so short a time that it is impossible to study them directly. The most that can be done is to make a slight memorandum at the time, and afterwards return at about the same hour and study what is permanent in the scene - all this for the purpose of fixing the effect in the memory.*[11]

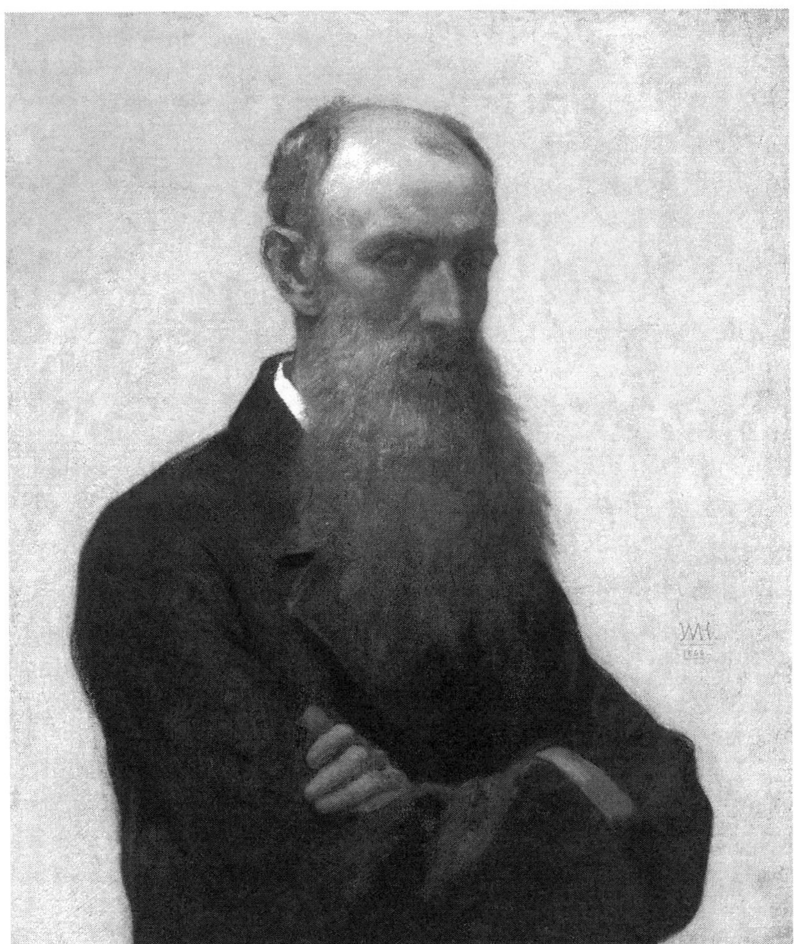

Self-Portrait by William Morris Hunt, 1866
The Metropolitan Museum of Art, New York

It is interesting to note that many of the nineteenth and early twentieth-century artists who wrote of visual memory did so as related to landscape painting. This was not exclusively the case, however, and those who wrote instructional manuals mentioned memory for landscape no more often than they did for other genre. But for a practicing artist, especially during the years when landscape painting moved increasingly out of doors, a trained visual memory became ever more essential. The atmospheric effects many artists were interested in painting were fleeting, and the camera, although helpful to some, was still mostly a small-scale, black and white medium. As mentioned earlier, these artists' motivations for landscape painting via memory were more related to picture-making than to literal recording. Additionally, the levels of accuracy and likeness expected by the public were, if not less, than at least different for landscape than for portraiture and figure painting.

That said, figure and portraiture were not left out of the memory-drawing picture entirely. Of the writings I have found on these aspects of memory drawing, Edgar Degas' comments seem to be the most often quoted. Bear in mind that there are many, slightly different versions of the following quote.

> *If I were to open an academy I would have a five-story building. The model would pose on the ground floor with the first-year students. The most advanced students would work on the fifth floor.*[12]

As related to training for portraiture specifically:

> *For portrait-studies, pose the sitter on the ground floor while the students work upstairs, so as to train them to remember shapes and never to paint directly.*[13]

Much like the aforementioned landscape painters, Degas had much to say on this subject because he was impressed with the connection between our memory and our imagination.

> *It is all very well to copy what you see; it is much better to draw what you only see in memory. There is a transformation during which the imagination works in conjunction with the memory. You only put down what made an impression on you, that is to say the essential. Then your memory and your invention are freed from the dominating influence of nature. That is why pictures made by a man with a trained memory who knows thoroughly both the masters and his own craft are almost always remarkable works; for instance, Delacroix.*[14]

The student should bear in mind that Degas never formally taught, and in my opinion his advice on these matters needs to be taken only generally, especially since they are often quoted out of their initial context. The main idea, however, that a trained visual memory was of immense help to the artist, stands without question.

As we have seen, these painters, as well as a number of other artists who wrote about memory, seem to have believed that true picture-making involved accurately studying the subject directly but then painting away from the subject through the use of one's memory. How often this was actually done, and to what degree, may never be fully known. Some do successfully paint in this way. More common though is that the artist's visual memory skills are put to use in speeding up the process when the live model is present as well as helping them adjust the painting after the model has gone.

Earlier I quoted Sir Joshua and his advice to use one's memory of the Antique and the Old Masters in order to help in composition. Later on in the second Discourse he offered the following practical advice for the student.

> *I would particularly recommend that after your return from the academy (where I suppose your attendance to be constant), you would endeavor to draw the figure by memory. I will even venture to add, that by perseverance in this custom, you will become able to draw the human figure tolerably correct, with as little effort of the mind as to trace with a pen the letters of the alphabet.*[15]

This was the same recommendation I was given when studying at various ateliers. It is also the basis of a number of visual memory-training systems, like the methods developed by Boisbaudran, Elizabeth Cavé and others.

Père Lecoq

The standard book on memory drawing was written in the mid-nineteenth-century by a French artist and teacher named Horace Lecoq de Boisbaudran. The original, from 1848, as well as the later editions are of course, long out of print, but they are now available once again for free online. His book, as we have it translated into English, is really a collection of three pamphlets. The relevant section, *The Training of the Memory in Art*, is a brief outline of his recommended visual memory-training process with the bulk of the text composed of the story of how he developed his system. Through the combined pamphlets he was also attempting to influence the way in which the French government conducted arts education. Although many artists had used their visual memory, and some had even written about it, Boisbaudran's book seems to have been the first to incorporate a systematic, step-by-step process designed specifically to teach memory drawing. Due to this, he may now be more well known for his book than the fact that he taught drawing to numerous painters including, Legros, Cazin, Fantin-Latour and sculptors Carpeaux and Rodin.

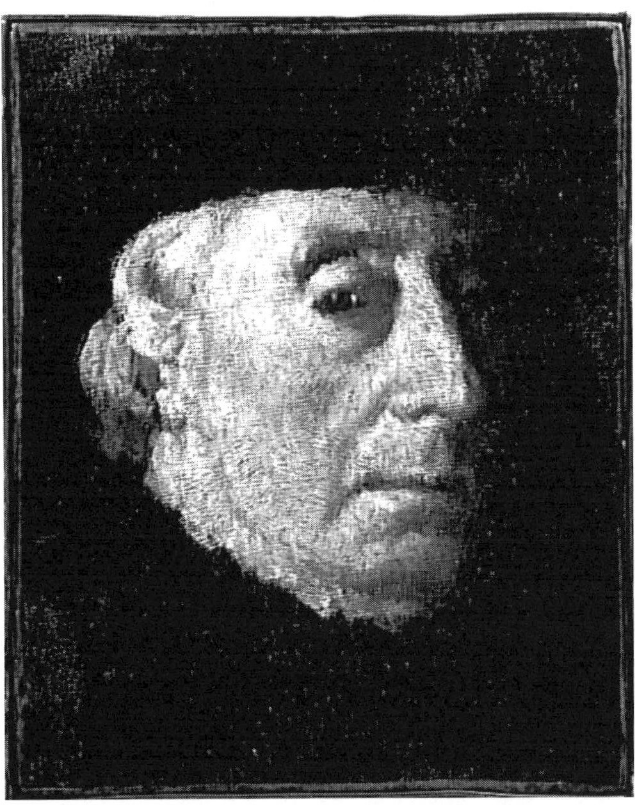

Self-Portrait by Horace Lecoq de Boisbaudran
Musée du Louvre, Paris

Père Lecoq, as Boisbaudran's students called him, begins his book by defining visual memory as "stored observation." I find that definition to be not only obvious but also quite profound. To observe takes conscious thought and effort; it is not simply an awareness of a fleeting impression. He then goes on to assure his readers that he has, *"No intention of letting unthinking memory work take the place of intelligence."* His stated objective is to cultivate the two equally. For our visual memory to be intelligent, our eye, as well as our memory, needs training. Training, in the sense Boisbaudran means, is largely directed by the pursuit of accuracy as a student.

> *And I take this opportunity of insisting upon this essentially important point, that it is this absolute fidelity of likeness to the model, this exactness and simplicity, which must be demanded of the beginner; for it is the only way to cultivate accuracy and naiveté of memory. It is only later, when the powers of correctness and precision have already been acquired, that he should be allowed to try and render a subject by interpretations, equivalents, and abstractions, in order to express its essential spirit, rather than its literal aspect.*[16]

Again, this time from the forward to his book:

> *Real progress in art, for the student and mature artist alike, consists in continually educating the eye to greater refinement of perception, and the hand to greater control and subtlety of execution; while the most frequent obstacle to progress is the forming of set habits of eye and hand, generally borrowed from others, for they necessarily interfere with the development of personal observation and self-expression.*[17]

Selwyn Image, a designer, whose family name befits that of an artist, wrote the introduction to the English translation of Boisbaudran's book. He had this to say about fidelity to nature and memory training:

> *Objection is sometimes raised to memory work, on the ground that it teaches students to draw out of their heads . . . Of this danger Boisbaudran was well aware, and his teaching is carefully designed to combat it. In memory work, as in ordinary work, he tells us, the first step in training is the practice of literal imitation. For upon this alone is built up the power of expressing exactly and completely the profounder* [sic] *and less literal impressions, which an artist receives from nature later on, as his personality develops and matures.*[18]

Image goes on to comment on the fact that proving the student's accuracy is difficult because the source has often been removed from view. This is one of the many reasons that memory work from master drawings, paintings and yes, even photographs, is of such great benefit - the result can be literally compared to the static source.

Boisbaudran recognized another benefit to memory drawing; that if studied properly it helps train the student to see the whole (also called the "big look" or the "unity of effect").

> [Drawings] *done from memory by young students, without the help of note or sketch of any kind, show a power of grasping a scene as a whole, of seizing its essential character and movement, rarely possessed even by mature artists. The*

weaknesses and faults in proportion or construction are just the things which are easily corrected from the model.[19]

Thinking and Unthinking?

As I mentioned before, Boisbaudran begins explaining the benefits of memory drawing by saying that he has *"no intention of letting unthinking memory work take the place of intelligence."*[20] Every time I read his book this clause strikes me as it clearly implies that there are two poles to our visual memory: one thinking and one not. To drive his point home he also tells us that the unthinking side is unintelligent. What is one to make of this? Millennia before Boisbaudran, Aristotle had a slightly different idea.

> *Memory, not merely of sensible, but even of intellectual objects, involves a presentation: hence we may conclude that it belongs to the faculty of intelligence only incidentally, while directly and essentially it belongs to the primary faculty of sense-perception.*[21]

From Ancient Greece onward the art world has been cursed with a controversy over whose version of art is derived from the intellect, whose is simply a poor imitation of nature, and whether one is better than the other. As it relates to art as well as to Boisbaudran's book, it is important to remember that the nineteenth-century was a time of great scientific exploration. New inventions such as the camera began to supplant artists, as the precipitous decline of a once-thriving market for painted miniature portraits showed. The attempt to accurately represent what one saw, in line, paint or marble, soon came to be looked down upon by some due to the apparent accuracy of the photo and the ease with which photographs were created.

This issue, among others, helped to focus the thinking in certain circles and gave them concrete ammunition. Additionally, the old idea that the artist's mind (their "intellect," in Boisbaudran's terms) should dominate their eye ("unthinking" in Boisbaudran's terms), ultimately led some to dispense with representation altogether. It is not surprising then that this climate greatly affected arts education, and in many ways the effects continue on today. But representation had, and still has, its adherents. Among those also there is at times a similar division. Just how far should accuracy be pursued? Is an artist better off following his mind or even his feelings? As we have seen, many of the landscape painters who wrote about memory did so principally because of its emotional aspects. With his statement Boisbaudran was appeasing both sides, and, in my opinion, he was correct to do so. One must not forget that a complete artist uses both eye and mind.

Boisbaudran's "Formula"

In his book, Boisbaudran initially divides visual memory training into form and color. In an appendix to a later edition he extends these divisions when outlining the basic process of analytical observation which were then to be applied to memory work. Since his comments on these subjects are highly important, I have reprinted them in Appendix I.

Boisbaudran had his students do memory exercises concurrent with their studies from life. He maintained that training the student's visual memory was not only a supplement to the student's main drawing lessons, it was an extension of them. The students were initially given a set of straight lines, angles and curves to memorize, followed by simple anatomical plates. Only after the student could accurately draw these from memory were they allowed to progress. The next task was to memorize more complex engravings, in ever decreasing amounts of time. Here Boisbaudran was trying to train his students to quickly observe and memorize fleeting images.

Copying in the Louvre was a time-honored tradition and many would say a necessary step in an artist's training. Boisbaudran agreed and required his students to do some of their Louvre copies via their memory. In fact, when asked to prove his method to the Commission of the École des Beaux-Arts, the task given to one of his students, Georges Bellenger, was to go to the Louvre and memorize Titian's *A Woman at Her Toilet* (the painting was then known as the portrait of *Laura de Dianti*). He was to draw it from memory, directly in front of the Commission. Below is his result, on the left, and the original Titian on the right.

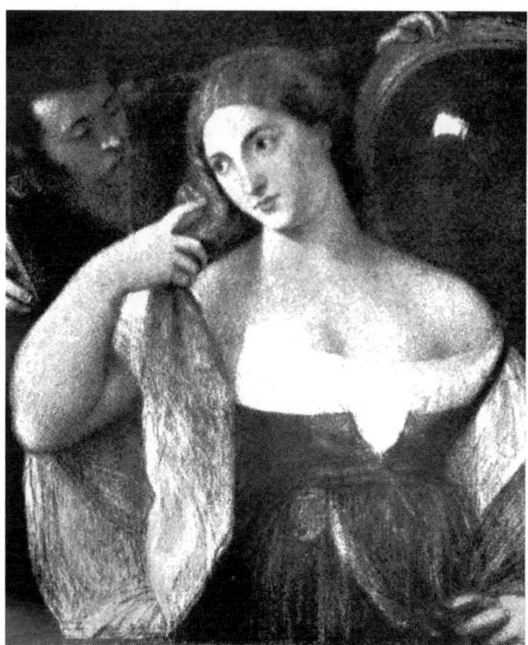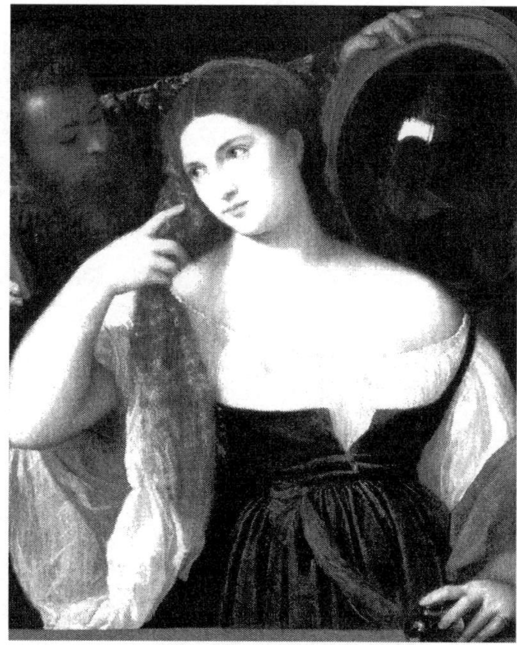

Boisbaudran somewhat deviated from his accuracy mandate when it came to drawing the day's figure model from memory, which was the next step in the memory drawing process. Here was his nod to the *Ideal*. Like many of his contemporaries, Boisbaudran believed the human figure to be visually imperfect. This takes us back to both of the Reynolds' quotes I mentioned earlier. Boisbaudran's students were to draw the figure from memory *and* be artistically, or imaginatively selective about it. However, this idealization through their memories was only to be done after they had demonstrated their ability to be consistently accurate in drawing the figure directly from life.

Although he left memory for color out of the first edition of his book, he included it in all of the later editions. His experiments with color memory led him to conclude that the students' abilities to memorize form did not match their abilities to memorize color. Very often, students seemed more *gifted* for one than the other.

The final part of the process, what he called *"the true artistic application of memory,"* was to memorize fleeting effects and moving figures. In an outdoor setting chosen for its beauty, Boisbaudran had nude and clothed models walk, run and stand before the students. Now and then he had the model stop when a beautiful pose or attitude was seen. When back in the studio a day or so later, the students would attempt to draw or paint from their memories whatever scene or pose had impressed them.

Boisbaudran's Influence

Boisbaudran's book was somewhat well received, and his students went on to teach others as well as to influence their contemporaries. Whistler, through his friends', Alphonse Legros and Fantin-Latour (both former Boisbaudran students), is but one prime example of this extended influence. There is evidence that at least some of Gérôme's and Gleyre's students practiced memory drawing as well. Thomas Eakins, who was a student of Gérôme and Bonnat, writes of his memory drawing experiences in a number of his letters.[22] The benefits of memory drawing became so widely known that eventually many state-run art schools in Britain and the U.S. incorporated it into their curriculum, even at times directly following Boisbaudran's teachings. However, the training at these schools was more often geared towards the decorative arts, or the arts and crafts, than what we now call the fine arts and therefore few took memory drawing as far as Boisbaudran had in mind.

As I mentioned above, Whistler is a good example of the impact Boisbaudran's teachings had. When studying contemporary accounts of Whistler from his friends and acquaintances it soon becomes clear that he made ample use of his trained memory in any number of his paintings. This was especially true for his *Nocturnes*. There are many stories of how he used his memory for some of his paintings. The following, as quoted from an early biography, is perhaps a prime example of these.

> *His method was to go out at night, and all his pupils or followers agree in this, stand before his subject and look at it, then turn his back on it and repeat to whoever was with him the arrangement, the scheme of color, and as much of the detail as he wanted. The listener corrected errors when they occurred, and, after Whistler had looked long enough, he went to bed with nothing in his head but his subject. The next morning, as he told his apprentice, Mrs. Clifford Addams, if he could see upon the untouched canvas the completed picture, he painted it; if not, he passed another night in looking at the subject. However, it was not two nights' observation alone, but the knowledge of a lifetime that enabled him to paint the Nocturnes. This power to see a finished picture on a bare canvas is possessed by all great artists. But the greater the artist the more he sees and the better he presents it.[23]*

Throughout Boisbaudran's book, he maintains that the student should always look to nature, eventually as filtered through the *Ideal* lens of the *Antique* as well as the Old Masters. In the end, this may best explain his goal of training "thinking" artists as opposed to "unthinking" copyists.

The First Method of Drawing that Teaches Anything

Boisbaudran's book was not the first book on memory drawing. That distinction may belong to Marie Elisabeth Blavot Boulanger Cavé and her book, *Drawing Without A Master: The Cavé Method for Learning to Draw from Memory*.[24] Madame Cavé's book is a set of lessons for young children. They were written as a collection of letters to her friend Julia, in order to help her educate her daughter in the art of drawing. The lessons in the book became known as *The Cavé Method*.

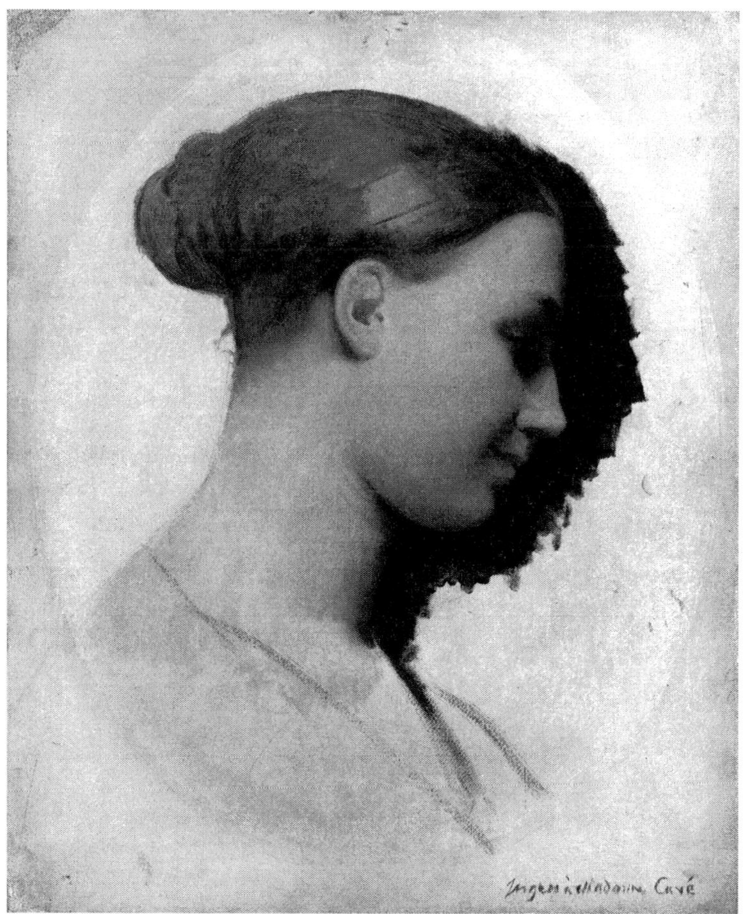

Portrait Study of Madame Cavé by Ingres, 1831-1834
The Metropolitan Museum of Art, New York

Elizabeth Cavé was an artist, and her first husband, Clément Boulanger, was a student of Ingres. For a time during that first marriage she was Delacroix's mistress as well. Although the affair did not last, she and Delacroix remained close. So close, in fact, that upon publication of her first book Delacroix wrote, in his review for the magazine, *Revue des Deux-Mondes*, *"Here is the first method of drawing that teaches anything."*[25] He also railed against the state-sponsored method of teaching children to draw via what we now call construction or concept.

> *Who does not remember the pages of noses, ears and eyes which afflicted our childhood? Those eyes, methodically divided into three perfectly equal parts-the central one occupied by the eyeball, which was represented by a circle; that inevitable oval the point of departure for drawing the head, which is neither oval nor round, as every one knows; in short, all those parts of the human body, copied endlessly and always separately, and requiring in the end a new Prometheus to construct therefrom a perfect man. Such are the notions beginners receive, and which are through life a source of error and confusion.*[26]

In essence, the Cavé Method is based upon observation which is then followed by memory. Like Boisbaudran, she believed that the artist must first learn how to perceive nature correctly, only then would they be able to correct nature's imperfections through a study of the Old Masters and a reliance on their memory. To do this properly, she advocated that the student begin their studies by tracing the outline of the subject onto a piece of translucent gauze which had been stretched over a frame. The tracing becomes the *proof.* The student then tries to draw the subject, using the traced proof as a teacher, oftentimes overlaying the drawing with it to check for accuracy. The next step, to be done on the same day, was to redraw the subject from memory which was then also checked with the proof. Finally, later that evening, the student was to do yet another memory drawing of the same subject, only this time the proof was not to be used. The main goal, of course, was to teach the student to draw, as Delacroix stated in his review, *"not the reproduction of the object as it is,* [construction, perspective, etc.] *but as it appears* [to the eye].*"*

Eventually the Cavé Method garnered enough praise that a report was given to the French Minister of the Interior by Felix Coitereau, an historical painter and the French Inspector-General of Fine Arts.[27] He witnessed the results of Madame Cavé's method and outlined them in his report. The students he reported on displayed:

1.   *A remarkable correctness in the ensemble and contour of a figure or any other object.*
2.   *A reproduction from memory scarcely distinguishable from the copy.*
3.   *Acquaintance with the masters. I have readily recognized Raphael, Holbein, and others, in the drawings from memory of Madame Cavé's pupils, and I thus conclude they have for themselves become familiar to a certain degree with the great masters.*
4.   *Finally, the idea of perspective; that is, that without having learned any of the rules of the science, pupils, in tracing from nature execute correctly the greatest difficulty in the art of perspective foreshortening.*

Robert Catterson-Smith and "Shut-Eye" Drawing

Robert Catterson-Smith was at the center of English arts education in the early twentieth-century. He was an artist as well and is sometimes referred to as "the forgotten Pre-Raphaelite" because of his working relationship with William Morris and Edward Burne-Jones. These artists also influenced him in the ways of the Arts and Crafts movement. Eventually he became an influential teacher of design and was headmaster at a number of art schools in Birmingham, England.[28]

Like Boisbaudran before him, Catterson-Smith used his young students as a testing-ground for his theories on memory drawing. The results also led to a book, titled, *Drawing from Memory and Mind Picturing*.[29] Catterson-Smith's task was to train young people in the art of design as used in industry, and he believed that memory drawing was integral to this mission.

However, unlike Boisbaudran, fidelity to what was directly observed was not a prerequisite. *"I contend that the effort to make* [a memory drawing] *is far better training than is gained, as a rule, by making a drawing directly from an object."*[30] He believed that the observation required to do a good memory drawing gave the student information that was more pertinent to the subject than what normally occurred when drawing directly. This kind of reasoning assumes that drawing, while observing, is a thoughtless act. In this respect he was in lock-step with those who fostered the idea that artists who initially pursued accuracy to nature were engaging in nothing more than mindless copying.

Catterson-Smith's innovation was something he called "shut-eye" drawing.

> [When commencing an exercise, and after a brief look at the subject,] *in order to secure concentration the student is required to shut his eyes and image in his mind's eye the object or design he is about to draw. When he sees mentally a sufficiently clear image - still keeping his eyes shut - he draws an outline in pencil on paper of the image he sees. Of course the lines do not join up correctly, but as a rule it is easy to see what is intended.*[31]

The goal of this procedure was not to make an accurate drawing with their eyes closed. Rather, it was to "develop the power of visualization," or mind picturing. Once a shut-eye drawing was completed, the student put the drawing away. He was then to do another drawing, this time with his eyes open.[32] Catterson-Smith is not clear in his book whether these open-eye drawings were to be done exclusively from memory or with occasional reference to nature.

When describing his shut-eye method, Catterson-Smith partially leans on Boisbaudran. "[Boisbaudran recommends that] *the student draw in the air with the finger the object he is thinking of; but I consider the pencil a much more precise tool than the finger."*[33] However, in his book, Boisbaudran states that students were not meant to actually draw with their eyes closed. They were to first trace with their finger what they were actually observing and then to shut their eyes and trace the image, again in the air with their finger. Unfortunately, Catterson-Smith's shut-eye drawing method would eventually lead some artists into Abstract Expressionism.[34]

Lutz's Approach: Verbal and Visual

Perhaps the most recent book on memory drawing is from the 1930's. It is called, *Practical Course in Memory Drawing* by E. G. Lutz.[35] It is now out of print, and as it is still under copyright, an online version is not yet available. Lutz takes a distinctly constructive, as well as a *faceted* approach to memory drawing. Faceting is a way to simplify the shapes of an object or scene.[36] He had previously written a number of other books in which he advised this same method of beginning a drawing.

Lutz defines two approaches to memory drawing as *verbal* and *visual,* and he further claims that the use of both speeds the process of forming the mental image of what one is attempting to remember. He describes the verbal approach as a way of remembering via the name and verbal description of the subject. As you will read in a moment, this is akin to construction. He defines the visual approach as a *sight-impression,* which is essentially

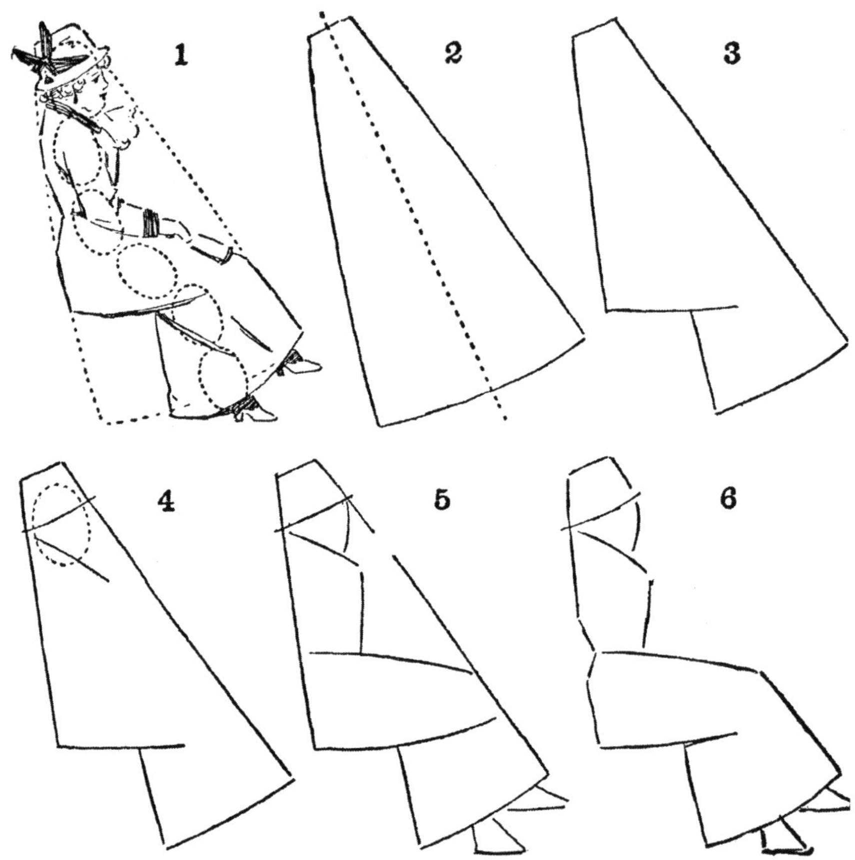

THE STEPS TAKEN IN THE ANALYSIS OF THE FIGURE
ILLUSTRATED ON THE OPPOSITE PAGE.

1. The general form is observed and the figure's height estimated.
2. The general action of the figure noticed.
3. The first change in the general form considered.
4. The position of the head is studied.
5. The form is broken up into smaller forms.
6. When the analysis has been carried this far, the attention may be given to the study of the small details.

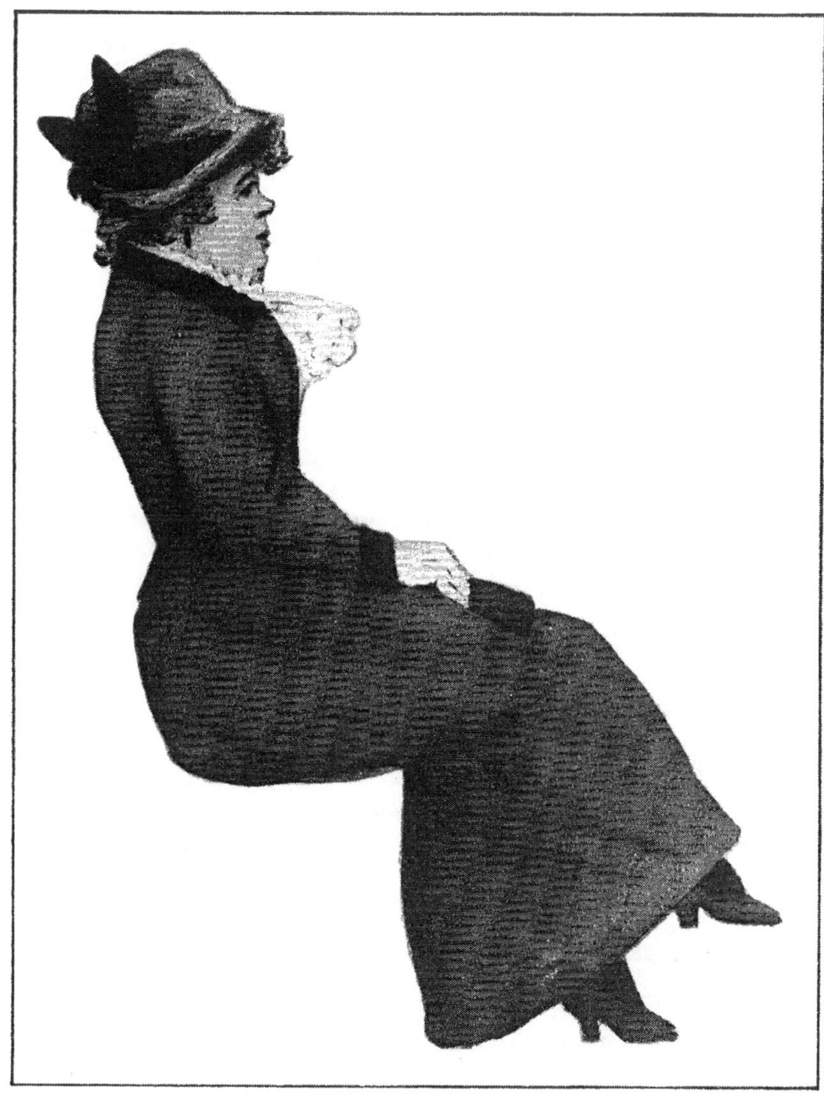

This image as well as the one on the preceding page come from
E. G. Lutz's book, *Practical Course in Memory Drawing.*

the un-examined image as it strikes our retina. His belief was that when artists are going through the process of doing a drawing from their memory, word-thoughts (construction) must be used.[37]

Construction drawing is often done by using cylinders and cubes to represent a set of shapes which make up the "construction" of whatever is being drawn. It emphasizes simplified, three-dimensional form. Lutz promotes this; however, he also uses construction in a two-dimensional sense, relative to faceting.[38] Through these two versions of construction, he teaches the student to simplify the observed shapes, from large to small. His book on memory drawing, like his other books, consists of numerous lessons showing objects and scenes rendered in this simplified 2- and 3-D fashion. It is meant to teach the student this type of seeing which is then supposed to aid them in their pursuit of memory drawing.[39]

Lutz's premise, that word-thoughts *must* be used when working from memory, is not something with which I completely agree. In my experience I find that it is definitely possible to draw or paint solely from one's memory of a sight-impression. To do this, however, serious training is needed. This is not to say that verbal analysis is useless. It is useful, but restricting one's memory training to that aspect alone is in reality simply learning to recall a formula.

1 Corot, as quoted in "Culture and Abroad." *Scribner's Monthly*. III.4 (February 1872): Page 501.

2 Crane, Walter. *Line & Form*. London: G. Bell , 1914. Page 214.

3 *Ibid.*, Pages 220-223.

4 *Ibid.*, Pages 220-223.

5 I am aware that the concept of inward vision, as related to memory drawing, was later pushed to the extreme by Robert Catterson-Smith's student Marion Richardson. In my opinion this is wholly unrelated to what Walter Crane had in mind and in its extreme form comes close to the automatism of the Abstract Expressionist action painters as well as to what is called automatic drawing.

6 Reynolds, Sir Joshua. *The Discourses of Sir Joshua Reynolds*. London: Kegan, Paul, Trench & Co. , 1884. Page 18.

7 Inness, George. "A Painter On Painting." *Harper's New Monthly Magazine*. February 1878: Page 458. Print. It is clear in these comments that Inness did not mean the photographic depiction of the scene nor the impression of it in the sense of the French Impressionists.

8 Inness, Jr., George. *Life, Art and Letters of George Inness*. New York: The Century Co., 1917.

9 See William Morris Hunt and Helen Mary Knowlton. *W.M. Hunt's Talks About Art*. London: Macmillan and Co. Limited, 1878. Print. and Hunt, William Morris., and Helen Mary Knowlton. *W.M. Hunt's Talks About Art: Second Series*. London: Macmillan and Co. Limited, 1883.

10 Hunt, William Morris., and Knowlton, Helen Mary. *W.M. Hunt's Talks About Art*. New York: Macmillan, 1878: Page 61.

11 Lawrence, Harold T. "A Painter of Idylls: Bruce Crane." *Brush and Pencil*. 11.1 (Oct. 1902): Pages 8-9.

12 *Degas* by Henri Hertz, Felix Alcan, Paris, 1920, as quoted in Gammell, R. H. Ives. *The Shop-talk of Edgar Degas*. Boston: University Press, 1961. Page 9. Robert Catterson-Smith, in his book, *Drawing From Memory and Mind Picturing* (1921) quotes the artist George Clausen, RA who attributes the idea to Boisbaudran, not Degas.

13 *Degas, Sa Vie et Son Oeuvre* by P.A. Lemoisne, Paul Brame, C.M. de Hauke aux Arts et Metiers Graphiques, Paris, 1946, as quoted in Gammell, R. H. Ives. *The Shop-talk of Edgar Degas*. Boston: University Press, 1961. Page 9.

14 *Souvenirs Sur Degas* by Georges Jeanniot, La Revue Universelle, 15 October and 15 November, 1933, Paris, as quoted in Gammell, R. H. Ives. *The Shop-talk of Edgar Degas*. Boston: University Press, 1961. Pages 8-9.

15 Reynolds, *op. cit.*, Page 18.

16 Boisbaudran, Horace Lecoq de. *The Training of the Memory in Art and the Education of the Artist*. London: Macmillan and Co. Limited, 1914. Pages 13-14.

17 *Ibid.*, pages IX-X.

18 Selwyn Image (translator) in Boisbaudran, Horace Lecoq de. *The Training of the Memory in Art and the Education of the Artist*. London: Macmillan and Co. Limited, 1914. Page 179.

19 *Ibid.*, Page 180.

20 Boisbaudran, *op. cit.*, Pages 13-14. Another possibility, besides the one I offer in the main text, is that by unthinking memory Boisbaudran meant hallucination. See Veerle Thielemans doctoral thesis, *The Afterlife of Images: Memory and Painting in Mid-Nineteenth Century France*, The Johns Hopkins University, 2001, in which she discusses Hippolyte Taine's concept of visual memory, voluntary hallucination and how it influenced contemporary artists of the time. Although Taine's theories were published after Boisbaudran's book, he may in fact be reacting to ideas like Taine's.

21 Aristotle, *On Memory and Reminiscence*, 350 BC, as translated by J.I. Beare, 13 Mar 2012. <http://classics.mit.edu/Aristotle/memory.html>

22 Reason, Akela. *Thomas Eakins and the Uses of History*. Philadelphia: University of Pennsylvania Press, 2010. Pages 91-95.

23 Pennell, Elizabeth, and Pennell, Joseph. *The Life of James McNeill Whistler*. London: J.B. Lippincott Company, 1911. Page 198.

24 Cavé, Madame Marie Elisabeth. *Drawing From Memory. The Cavé Method for Learning to Draw From Memory*. London: G.P. Putnam's Sons, 1886.

25 *Ibid.*, Page 5.

26 *Ibid.*, Page 6.
27 *Ibid.*, Page 19.
28 'Robert Sidney Catterson-Smith MA', *Mapping the Practice and Profession of Sculpture in Britain and Ireland 1851-1951*, University of Glasgow History of Art and HATII, online database 2011 [http://sculpture.gla.ac.uk/view/person.php?id=msib4_1206027300, accessed 15 Jul 2012]
29 Catterson-Smith, Robert. *Drawing From Memory and Mind Picturing.* London: Sir Isaac Pitman & Sons, 1921.
30 *Ibid.*, Page 7.
31 *Ibid.*, Page 13.
32 *Ibid.*, Pages 25-26.
33 *Ibid.*, Page 26.
34 See footnote #5.
35 Lutz, E. G. *A Practical Course in Memory Drawing.* New York: C. Scribner's sons, 1936.
36 See Appendix III in this volume for more information about curved versus faceted drawing.
37 *Ibid,.* Page 4.
38 In my experience spending time learning to simplify observed forms, in the way Lutz teaches as part of memory drawing exercises, may largely be a waste of time. If the student is taught to draw this way while in front of the live model, it will already be a habit. On the other hand, if the student is taught to draw with a more curved-based approach, then changing to flat lines simply for memory drawing will be a hinderance.
39 See Appendix III for more information about curved versus faceted drawing.

·Science·

Everyone has a photographic memory, some just don't have film.   -Stephen Wright

A cursory knowledge of how we recognize what we see and how we recall those images provides an interesting background to the subject of memory drawing. Numerous books and articles have been written on these issues and readers should be aware that the science is still not completely settled. It may never be to everyone's satisfaction.

Is Seeing Comprehending?

Before we look at visual memory specifically, it is helpful to understand how we visually perceive. In fact, because our visual memory is said to be linked to our visual perception, there may not be a clear division between the two. There are those who maintain that when we mentally connect something we see with some form of understanding of what it is, only then do we truly perceive it.

After we were born each of us had to learn how to see. A more accurate statement might be that we had to learn how to recognize what we were seeing. Our visual acuity developed through use and physical growth, but our recognition developed through trial and error, i.e. learning. Though distinct, the processes occur in concert with each other.

Research has shown that we are born seeing in shades of grey and able to focus only about ten inches away. Weeks later we begin to notice movement, to follow it with our heads, and eventually with just our eyes. At about four months of age our ability to observe really ramps up and we start to see in full color as well as to coordinate our eyes with our hands by touching what we look at. Additionally, once all of our senses begin to respond to our intents, they seem to share information. It seems that both motion and touch help our brains learn to recognize what our eyes are seeing.[1] Although the main wiring of our visual comprehension is mostly complete by the time we turn fifteen, the process really never stops.

True perception creates a clear memory. But more often than not, this memory, like most initial memories, will be fleeting unless we dwell upon it long enough and then return to it again. Our mind forms new memories continually, and where these memories get routed (short-term, working or long-term) is also an ever-changing process. This ability to remember information, is termed *brain plasticity*, and this is partly why we can remember and learn new things over the entire course of our lifetime. Age does play a part in this ability but not nearly as much as was once thought. A twenty-year-old may remember more and with greater clarity, but if you have reached the age of eighty, do not despair, all is not lost.

I maintain that acquiring a good visual memory requires that one has first attained good visual perception skills. Unfortunately, there is a debate as to exactly how those perception skills are best learned. Saul McLeod, a psychology lecturer at Wigan and Leigh College, explains:

> *A major theoretical issue on which psychologists are divided is the extent to which perception relies directly on the information present in the stimulus. Some argue that perceptual processes are not direct, but depends on the perceiver's expectations and previous knowledge as well as the information available in the stimulus itself.*[2]

Is perception based upon what is observed with no preconceptions imposed upon it, or is it dependent, at least in part, upon what the observer's mind expects to see? At this point in time there is no clear answer. It is interesting to note, however, that learning to draw is typically approached via these same two paths, direct and to a greater or lesser degree, indirect. Regardless of which option you side with, learning to draw is also learning to see.

Bottom-Up or Top-Down?

With the preceding division in mind, the direct path to learning to draw is learning to perceive through direct observation. This path is considered to be *bottom-up processing*. In other words, the brain's perception of the observed image begins with the observed image itself.[3] Perception using the bottom-up model does not rely upon a visual understanding of what the object actually is (an apple, a chair, etc.). Rather, it is concerned with the visual properties of the object independent of the object's classification.

The other path to learning to draw is more of an indirect one. This path tends to begin with an idea, a preconceived view or an association, whether the artist is always conscious of it or not. The idea can be based upon many things: construction, form, concept, anatomy or any combination of them. These beginnings are a set of learned principles, which in many cases were originally based upon observed fact. These then become a kind of prior knowledge about what is being observed. The brain begins with them, as opposed to the observed image itself, by presupposing those principles onto its perception of the image. Cognitive psychologists, call this kind of perception *top-down processing*. It is also known as a constructivist or indirect theory of perception.[4]

Although I have put them in terms of learning to draw or see, these theories of visual perception comprise the two standard viewpoints of visual-perceptual learning.[5] Additionally, if we think in terms of representational art history and instruction, it soon becomes clear that both models are really parts of a whole. The direct model presumes ideal viewing conditions, where the subject is always present and the artist is dispassionately recording what he sees. When your teacher says, "Look at the shape," she is telling you to use the direct model of seeing. The indirect model is advantageous when the viewing conditions are not perfect or when the artist is more interested in drawing from a concept or their imagination. Even when a model is present, your teacher may refer to anatomy or construction. These references imply an indirect model. Whether it is best to learn to draw exclusively via one or the other, will have to be up to the student or their teacher.

The Whole is Something Besides the Parts[6]

This brief foray into the science of visual perception would be incomplete without some mention of gestalt theory. Gestalt is a German word that is difficult to define in English. For our purposes it basically means *form* or *shape,* and in this context it is further defined as *a unified whole.* Scientists began to examine the idea of gestalt, relative to perception, in the early nineteen-tens although many aspects of it have been known for millennia. Both Aristotle and Leonardo's writings contain observations which Gestaltists would recognize.

By the middle of the nineteenth-century, the theory began to have a significant impact on some in the visual arts, most notably many of the Impressionist movement as well as abstract painters like Paul Klee and Wassily Kandinsky.[7] The theory gave artists scientific proof for what they were attempting to do with their art.

> *One principal claim of Gestalt psychology is that, in perception, the whole precedes the parts . . . local structures or parts are perceived only by a slow, secondary process that relies on focal attention.*[8]

Despite the fact that abstract artists are most often associated with gestalt theory, numerous aspects of it apply to representational artists. Of note are the principles of simultaneous contrast, figure/ground relationships and most importantly, holistic seeing. Although these concepts had their origins centuries earlier, gestalt psychologists were the first to systematically study them.

Essentially, simultaneous contrast explains that our perception of a value or a color is affected by its surroundings. The reverse is also true. Imagine an apple tree, fully leafed out but with only one red apple on it. In varying degrees, our perception of the color of the red apple will be different than it would be if the apple were on a white background.[9]

Regarding figure/ground, many artists are taught to mentally separate the shape of the subject from the shape of the background. I learned to identify these abstract shapes as *positive shapes* and *negative shapes* (the negative shape being the background). In gestalt theory they are called *figure* and *ground.*[10]

The principle of holistic seeing is simply seeing the whole of the image as opposed to seeing it in a piecemeal fashion. I was taught to call holistic seeing, the *"big look."*

Aristotle, the author of this section's heading, is often misquoted to read, *the whole is greater than the sum of the parts.* The difference is subtle but both versions are true. The *whole* visual image of a scene is at the same time different and greater than its constituent parts. This concept is the basis for something called the gestalt effect, which is defined as, *"The form-generating capability of our senses, particularly with respect to the visual recognition of figures and whole forms instead of just a collection of simple lines and curves."*[11]

The image below is perhaps the most common example of the gestalt effect. It was first created by Danish psychologist Edgar Rubin and it is variously known as the *Rubin's vase* or the *faces-vases illusion*. Many elementary school art classes use this illusion to teach their students the concepts of figure/ground and holistic seeing.

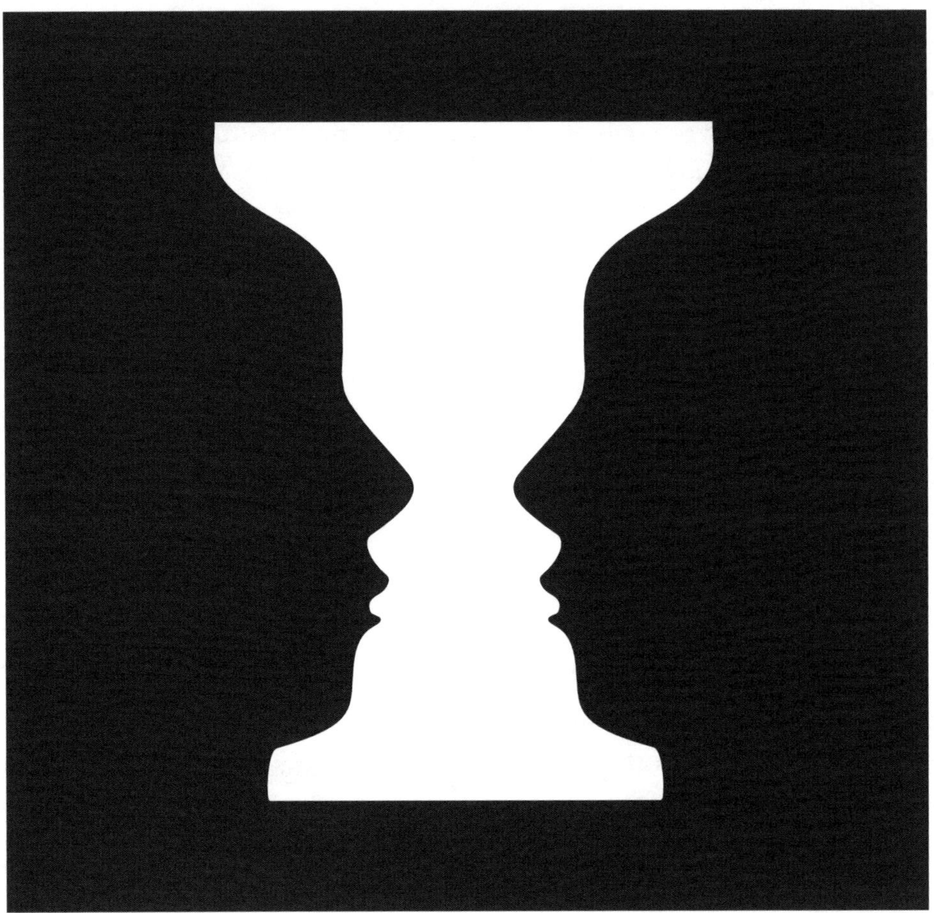

One can then state as a fundamental principle: When two fields have a common border, and one is seen as figure and the other as ground, the immediate perceptual experience is characterized by a shaping effect which emerges from the common border of the fields and which operates only on one field or operates more strongly on one than on the other.[12]

Gestalt theory is now thought by some to be far too vague[13] and there are a number of other theories which seek to explain how our mind perceives the world.

Seen and Unseen

Relative to recalling visual memories the main question is, are they perceived mentally as images by our minds in the same way that our minds grasp what we actually observe? In other words, do they form a literal picture in our mind? Or are they a mental construct of what we know about what we are trying to recall, a conceptual description of the image?

Aristotle and Descartes[14] are said to have believed the former. This view is called the "picture theory of mental imagery," and inasmuch as it is possible to test this, scientists generally accepted this view as fact until relatively recently. Like many of the concepts in this chapter, it is undergoing debate among those studying the issue.[15]

Given my experience with memory drawing, I lean towards Aristotle's viewpoint. The accuracy and specificity possible when one is trained in memory drawing is astounding. In my opinion, it is too great to simply be explained by our brain's ability to describe something visual only in knowledge-based terms. That said, the fact is that our brain thrives on visual structure and hierarchy; it cannot help but to categorize what we perceive. Unfortunately, a definitive answer to these questions may never be known. Perhaps the bottom-up and top-down models of perception meet in middle. In other words, they may meet in our memories as our minds go through the process of recalling them.

Dual Coding

Numerous studies have shown that images are remembered far more effectively than words. Scientists call this the "pictorial superiority effect."[16] To help you strengthen this ability, I will have you spend some time trying to memorize the images without thinking about their descriptive qualities in the exercise chapters which follow. However, what is more interesting is that combining relevant words or simple descriptions along with the image increases ones ability to recall the image more than just thinking about the image on its own.[17] Of course the key here is relevancy. The words need to mean something relative to the image.

Many cognitive psychologists believe that our minds store memories using two systems, the visual and the verbal. When both systems are used at once, the memory is then considered to be "dual coded."[18] Whether or not the specifics of this theory are proved to be correct, the main principle is sound. Combining relevant verbal observations or descriptions about a scene with visual observation helps our brain to store those observations in our long-term memory. It also enhances our ability to recall them.

That, of course, is not the full story. There are stages which our mind goes through in order to memorize something. These stages are aspects of what is called "depth of processing."[19] There are a number of other theories which seek to explain how our mind perceives the world. It is no surprise that the deeper an observation is processed the better we will be able to recall it later on. It makes sense that to deeply process something is to analyze it. In most instances this is true. But our minds can also deeply process some observations without conscious analysis. Observing something out of the ordinary, even for a very brief period of time, tends to result in a memory that goes beneath the surface. The key to this rests in our experience of the observation along with the skills we bring to the situation. As an art student you are training your observational abilities, hopefully on a daily basis. This training alone will help to improve your visual memory because you look at things differently and more deeply than a non-artist would.

It might seem as if the previous sections of this chapter would be of little, practical use for the process of memory-drawing training. In fact, they are integral to it. Once again, the main theme is whether it is most effective to memorize what you are seeing or to memorize what you know about what you are seeing. Relative to these options, memorizing what you see is simply focusing or fixating your attention exclusively on the subject in a non-discerning way and for a period of time, then, looking away and trying to recall it in your mind or even describing it verbally out loud.

Memorizing what you know is comprised of focusing your attention on the subject while thinking about what its characteristics are. After that, when trying to recall it in your mind, you are more specifically reconstructing it based upon what you know it to be.

As I showed in the chapter on history, both approaches were used in the past. From experience I conclude that the most effective long-term approach is actually a combination of the two. However, learning these two approaches as separate skills, at least in the early stages, is paramount. Once the student's mind is able to separate their perceptions from their knowledge, a more intentionally blended approach becomes effective.

Of One or Two Minds?

When it comes to actually doing a memory drawing, there is some debate. It seems that the issue is whether one can mentally attend to both the drawing in progress as well as to the visual memory at the same time. Does the act of drawing switch the brain out of memory mode so far that the memory as a reference is no longer specifically applicable? Some studies seem to bear this out.[20] If true, the reference point is then more conceptual or association-based. Those conceptual-associations are often more generic than specific (e.g., in general, an apple might be spherical and red, but for a specific apple, how spherical and exactly which red).

It is true that non-artists (both children and adults) operate in a conceptual-association mode when trying to draw, even if the subject is directly in front of them.[21] Therefore I have no trouble believing that they are as incapable of accurately drawing from their memory as they are of accurately drawing from life. Why would they be able to? They cannot perceive as an artist does because they have had no training. However, trained representational artists who are also trained in memory drawing are able to retain both the conceptual associations and the image memory in their minds while doing the drawing. To do this they do not rely on associations alone. I have seen, and done, too many memory drawings to think otherwise.

Photographic Memory

Before we leave the science of perception and memory behind we need to take a look at photographic memory. Dictionary.com defines photographic memory as, *the ability to recall images with vividness bordering on actual visual perception; total recall.*[22] Google however, defines it as, *the ability to remember information or visual images in great detail.*[22] People who say they have a photographic memory may prefer Dictionary.com's definition although Google's is likely closer to what they claim to have.

The fact is that there has only been one proven case of photographic memory and even that is questionable.[24] The researcher, Harvard scientist Charles Stromeyer III, and his subject, a Harvard teacher, ended up marrying each other. She was never tested again.

Some savants, known as visual savants, are also believed to have a photographic memory. Stephen Wiltshire is perhaps the most famous.[25] While there is no doubt that Stephen and others like him possess a remarkable ability, it is difficult to determine how photographically accurate it is. Stephen's drawings are not exact copies of the subject and we do not know whether this is intentional or not.

The closest thing to a real photographic memory is something called eidetic memory.[26] Eidetickers claim to continue *seeing* a very detailed image after the object or scene is removed from their sight. Researchers prove this ability by using eye tracking equipment.[27] This equipment allows the subject's gaze is tracked while their eyes look at a photograph. The photograph is then removed and the subject is asked to *look* at the scene again, as if it was still present, and their eyes are tracked once again. How accurately these tracks match, in part, determines whether the person is considered to be an eidetic. It is thought that less than 10% of children have this ability and that almost no adults do.

Do you have an eidetic memory? Take this online test to find out: http://www.open. edu/openlearn/body-mind/psychology/take-the-photographic-memory-test

A Self-Made Eidetic?

Do artists with a trained visual memory perceive visual imagery after the literal image is gone, like an eidetic does? At present, proving this is difficult because so few artists have taken the time to improve their visual memories. To my knowledge none of them have been scientifically studied. Furthermore, one difference between a trained visual memory and eidetic memory is that eidetic memory is only short term, somewhat like an afterimage.[28] In my own case the answer to this question is both yes and no. What I *see* most often is more of a highly accurate impression, akin to a gut feeling that occurs when my drawing deviates from my memory of the scene.

All of us but those with a visual handicap have a built-in ability to accurately recall visual perceptions, if only for a short time. How accurate are perceptions are, along with how attentive we are to them, determine how well we can recall them at a later time. Once again, the first goal of memory-drawing training is to teach the artist how to accurately perceive. The process of perceiving and attending to those perceptions in specific ways actually helps move those perceptions into long term memory.

1 Christopher G., Thomas, "Project Prakash Enlightens Our Understanding of Vision." N.p., n.d. 1 Feb 2012. <http:// www.nei.nih.gov/news/scienceadvances/discovery/project_prakash.asp>.
2 McLeod, S.A., "Simply Psychology; Visual Perception." N.p., 2007. 3 Feb 2012. <www.simplypsychology. org/perception-theories.html>.
3 *Ibid.*
4 *Ibid.*

5 "Perceptual Learning." *Wikipedia, The Free Encyclopedia.* Wikimedia Foundation, Inc. 17 Nov. 2011. <http://en.wikipedia.org/wiki/Perceptual_learning>.

6 Aristotle, Metaphysics, 350 BC, as translated by W. D. Ross, 23 Mar 2012. <http://classics.mit.edu//Aristotle/metaphysics.html>.

7 Behrens, Roy R. "Art, Design and Gestalt Theory." *Leonardo*, Vol. 31, No. 4 (1998), 299-303.

8 Pomerantz, James R. "Colour as a Gestalt: Pop Out with Basic Features and with Conjunctions" *Visual Cognition* , Vol. 14 (2006). Pages 621-622.

9 See Chevreul, Michel Eugène. *The Laws of Contrast of Colour.* Translated by John Spanton. London: Routledge, Warne, and Routledge, 1861.

10 Koffka, Kurt "Perception: An Introduction to the Gestalt-theorie" *Psychological Bulletin*, 19 (1922), 531-585. For the origin of the terms, see Edgar Rubin, Synsoplevede Figurer, (1915) and in English, http://www.psy.ku.dk/om/Historie/figure_and_ground_at_100/JLPind-Psychologist.pdf/.

11 "Gestalt Effect." *Wikipedia, The Free Encyclopedia.* Wikimedia Foundation, Inc. 23 Mar. 2012. <http://en.wikipedia.org/wiki/Gestalt_effect>.

12 Rubin, Edgar, *Synsoplevede Figurer*, (1915) and in English, http://www.psy.ku.dk/om/Historie/figure_and_ground_at_100/JLPind-Psychologist.pdf/.

13 ". . . the physiological theory of the Gestalts has fallen by the wayside, leaving us with a set of descriptive principles, but without a model of perceptual processing. Indeed, some of their "Laws" of perceptual organization today sound vague and inadequate. What is meant by a "good" or "simple" shape, for example?" -Bruce, V., Green, P. & Georgeson, M. (1996). *Visual perception: Physiology, psychology and ecology.* New York: Psychology Press, 2003. Page 127.

14 Descartes, René, and Cottingham, John. *Descartes: Meditations on First Philosophy: With Selections from the Objections and Replies.* Cambridge: Cambridge University Press, 1996.

15 For either side of the issue, see Kosslyn, Thompson and Ganis (2006), *The Case for Mental Imagery*, Oxford University Press and Pylyshyn, Z. W. (2003), "*Seeing and Visualizing: It's Not What You Think*," MIT Press/Bradford Books.

16 Levie, W. H., & Hathaway, S. N. (1988). "Picture Recognition Memory: A Review of Research and Theory," *Journal if Visual Literacy.* 8(1). 1988. Page 6.

17 Kunen, Seth and Duncan, Edward M., "Do Verbal Descriptions Facilitate Visual Inferences?" *The Journal of Educational Research* , Vol. 76, No. 6 (Jul. - Aug., 1983). Pages 370-373.

18 Paivio, Allan. *Mental Representations: A Dual Coding Approach,* New York: Oxford University Press, 1990. Pages 53-83.

19 Craik and Lockhart (1972), "Levels of Processing: A Framework for Memory Research." Journal of Verbal Learning and Verbal Behaivior 11: 671-684.

20 McMahon, Jennifer A. "An Explanation for Normal and Anomalous Drawing Ability and Some Implications for Research on Perception and Imagery." *Visual Arts Research.* 28.1(55) (2002): 38-52.

21 Konkle, Talia, Timothy Brady, George A. Alvarez, and Aude Olivia. "Conceptual Distinctiveness Supports Detailed Visual Long-Term Memory for Real-World Objects." *Journal of Experimental Psychology: General.* 139(3). Aug (2010).

22 "Photographic memory." Dictionary.com's 21st Century Lexicon. Dictionary.com, LLC. 12 Jun. 2012. <Dictionary.com http://dictionary.reference.com/browse/photographic memory>.

23 "What is a Photographic Memory?" *Google.com.* 20 Nov. 2011. <http://google.com/>.

24 Stromeyer, C. F., Psotka, J. (1970). "The Detailed Texture of Eidetic Images". *Nature* 225 (5230): 346–349.

25 http://www.stephenwiltshire.co.uk.

26 "eidetic image." Encyclopædia Britannica. Encyclopædia Britannica Online Academic Edition. Encyclopædia Britannica Inc., 2012. Web. 26 May. 2012. <http://www.britannica.com/EBchecked/topic/180955/eidetic-image>.

27 "Eye tracking." Wikipedia. Web. 26 May. 2012. <http://en.wikipedia.org/wiki/Eye_tracking>.

28 An afterimage is a visual image or other sense impression that persists after the stimulus that caused it is no longer operative; also called a *photogene.* "Afterimage." Dictionary.com Unabridged. Random House, Inc. 12 Jun. 2012. <Dictionary.com http://dictionary.reference.com/browse/afterimage>. To experience this yourself, see: http://psylux.psych.tu-dresden.de/i1/kaw/diverses%20Material/www.illusionworks.com/html/afterimage.html.

·Process·

Thus, I name a stone, I name the sun, the things themselves not being present to my senses, but their images to my memory. . . . I name the image of the sun, and that image is present in my memory. For I recall not the image of its image, but the image itself is present to me, calling it to mind.[1]

The scientific background could go on for volumes, but let's get down to some of the practical ways in which you can improve your visual memory.

Almost any kind of visual-memory training will have some benefit and even a less than regular regimen will prove somewhat effective. Therefore, if you do no more than the examples I give in this book, or even a portion of them, you will be steps ahead from where you currently are. However, it should come as no surprise that a greater level of commitment will be far more effective than a lesser one. Be aware at the outset that acquiring a high level of visual-memory skill will take a lot of attentive practice and, like most endeavors, the more you put into it, the more you will get out of it. As such it is best to consider your visual-memory training a lifelong pursuit. With that in mind, the advice I gave near the end of the introduction still stands.

Remember, too, that these exercises are just that, exercises. They are meant to help you improve your visual memory, not necessarily provide you with a single system that you will use all of the time in the real world. You might use one or more of the following techniques but it is up to you to figure out which ones are effective for you and which are not. On the other hand, over time many of the systematic aspects will become an automatic habit and that is a good thing.

Shape, Value, Color

The exercises in the following chapters are separated into three categories: shape, value and color. Our minds perceive these characteristics differently and therefore you will have an easier time training your memory for them separately.

Source Images

As I mentioned in an earlier chapter, the simple act of drawing something helps you remember it. This can make things difficult because your end goal is to recall something you have previously seen, not something you have previously drawn. To most effectively do this you need to find visual sources which you have not created yourself or had at least created long ago. With the exception of color, I have given you examples of what to look for through the exercises in the book. Ongoing examples may be found through the links on this website: http://www.memorydrawing.com.

Trained artists know that the color range of their paints (called a gamut) is more restricted than what is seen in nature. This gamut is also different than what is seen in the colors printed in a color book or on a website. You have to be able to mix the color you are seeing, converted into the gamut-range your paints can achieve. If your chosen medium cannot hit those colors, you are wasting your time. This is especially important for memory drawing. I will write more about this in the chapter on color but for now you should be aware that you will need to create your own color sources. If you are attending an art school, your teacher may provide them for you or you might consider teaming up with another student in order to exchange sources. After a lot of practice painting directly what you see, and with memory drawing, you will become more adept at adjusting to the gamut of your medium. At that point images on a printed page or website will be less troublesome.

Attention

Perhaps the most important advice I can give is that you pay attention. Your mind has to be actively engaged in the process or it is highly unlikely that your observations will pass beyond your working memory. Try to be aware of whether or not your mind is wandering. When you notice this happening, refocus your attention or perhaps take a break.

Feedback

Part of the process is checking your work for errors. For many of the exercises I will have you draw on tracing paper. You will then correct it with a colored pencil. As you go through the next session of any particular exercise be mindful of your previous errors and their corrections. Over time this act will help you hone in on any consistent problems. This knowledge will then allow you to actively correct your mannerisms.

These tracing paper/colored pencil corrections work well for shape, but for value and color you will have to take notes of your errors instead. It is best to do this right on the your attempt at the exercise itself.

Journal and Review

Not every technique will work equally well for everyone and the best way to discover what works for you is to keep track of what you are doing. In order to do that you will want to keep a file of all of your memory work. Along with noting your errors, try to write down what processes you followed. Every month, or so, you should go back over them to determine what aspects need additional effort. Are your memory drawings consistently too wide or too tall? Are they usually too dark? When reviewing, ask yourself these questions and others. Then, while you are working on your exercises, pay more attention to those aspects which you find need improvement.

Doubling Down

Beginning students tend to start out poorly but then quickly pick up their speed and accuracy. Then, after serious effort, their improvement levels off. This is variously called a "plateau" or "hitting a wall," just like in athletic training. When this happens the best thing to do is to go back over your old exercise attempts and focus on the ones where you made the most mistakes. You may also find that reducing your observational time and/or using a source which is far more complicated than you are used to will "get you over the hump."

Start Staring

In order to most effectively train your brain's dual-coding abilities, I will ask you to memorize the images in two ways: staring and analyzing. Staring, for our purposes, is an active process. When you do this you will be intentionally thinking about the image while trying not to actually analyze it. Stare into the center of the shape, or slightly away, and take the image in as a whole. Don't worry if you find this very difficult at first, your mind wants to analyze. The mental energy it takes to focus without analyzing is tremendous and early on the act of doing it may actually become your focus. Persist and you will find it easier. Successfully staring in this way seems to be easier for value and color than for shape.

Analysis

Accurate shape is determined by comparison to other shapes. Accurate value is determined by comparison to other values and accurate color is determined by comparison to other colors. When you analyze for the purposes of memory training, the main questions you will ask yourself are almost always comparison, or relationship-based.

Association and Caricature

We recall images better when we can associate them with something we already know. For example, let's say that you are trying to memorize a shape that looks somewhat similar to a stop sign. Note that characteristic -it looks like a stop sign- and then try to observe and memorize how it differs from a stop sign. When it is time to draw from that memory you will instantly recall the stop sign image and therefore have a head start.

Caricature is similar except that you mentally exaggerate features or entire scenes in order to help make it memorable. These caricatures are hopefully more memorable than the actual observations themselves and the effort is then more directed towards memorizing how they differ from the caricature.

Rehearsing

Imagine trying to remember a phone number. Typically, you would say it aloud, over and over again until you think that you know it. That act is rehearsal. Memory-drawing rehearsal is naturally a bit different. One of the basic processes is to close your eyes and try to imagine the source image in your mind. If you are memorizing a shape, you might mentally draw it in your mind while your eyes are closed. Or you might verbally describe the object or scene out loud. The main idea is to get the image from your short-term memory into your long-term memory. Recreating the object in your mind, or through your audible words, helps you do that.

Finger Tracing

Tracing is actually a form of rehearsal and there are two ways to do it. The first is done while you are looking directly at the image. Physically trace over the shape with your finger in the air. The other way is to close your eyes and trace it in the air as if you are still seeing it.[2] It is this process which will partially help you recall the *sight-impression*, as E. G. Lutz termed it. You should do both of these options a number of times when you are observing the source image. While tracing is obviously applicable to shape, you can also use your finger to point out value and color observations as well.

Chunking

Let's go back to that phone number I mentioned on the previous page. Have you ever wondered why local phone numbers in the U.S. are seven digits long and are divided like this: 315-2743.[3] The answer to that is a long story which essentially comes down to chunking. It seems that our brains can only store around seven items in its working memory.[4] These seven items are more easily remembered if they are chunked into groups. So, 315-2743 is an easier number to remember than 3152743. Adding an area code into the mix complicates things a bit but those codes are still chunked into three digits. Furthermore they are chunked into distinct geographical regions. For instance, if you live near Minneapolis you know that its area code is 612. That information becomes a known chunk which you mentally tag onto any new phone number that is local to you.

Chunking works a bit differently in the visual realm, but the concept is still valid. As you analyze your source image it is helpful to categorize similar aspects of it. Take a look at the image below. Notice that there are three straight lines and that the remaining part is curved. This description is but one example of visual chunking.

1 Saint Augustine, Bishop of Hippo. *The Confessions of Saint Augustine, Book X.* Translated by Edward Bouverie Pusey.
2 Levin, Ghatala, DeRose, and Makoid. "Image Tracing: An Analysis of Its Effectiveness in Children's Pictorial Discrimination Learning". *Journal of Experimental Child Psychology*, 23, 1, 78-83, Feb 77.
3 Anon user. "Technology: Why Did Bell Labs Create Phone Numbers of 7 Digits - 10 Digits?." *Quora.* N.p.. Web. 23 Oct 2012. <http://www.quora.com/Technology/Why-did-Bell-Labs-create-phone-numbers-of-7-digits-10-digits>.
4 Miller, George A. "The Magical Number Seven, Plus or Minus Two: Some Limits on Our Capacity for Processing Information." *Psychological Review*. 63. (1956): 81-97.

·Shape·

Thinking is more interesting than knowing, but not so interesting as looking. -Goethe

Shape is often the beginning of artistic representation. It is also the beginning of visual memory training.

For our purposes I will initially define shape based upon its two-dimensional aspects only. Those of you who are sculptors will want to follow along as well, because even though sculpture is a three-dimensional medium, training your visual memory using two-dimensional observations is a sound starting point. Matthew Collins and I will further advise sculptors in the chapter on sculptural memory.

Seeing and Knowing

The concepts of "directly seeing" and "indirectly knowing" sum up the basis for almost all of the divisions outlined in the first part of this book. Although I was trained primarily through direct observation (i.e., no construction, and anatomy was used simply as an important reference), even the most ardent observer among my teachers would have agreed that a knowledge of what one sees can be immensely helpful when memory training.

We all know, for instance, what the basic shapes of commonly seen objects are and it is only natural that we rely on this knowledge to some degree. We do, however, need training in how to correctly observe the specifics in order to properly place the exact image in our memory. Fortunately, most representational art schools tend to teach this kind of seeing. But that is the easy stuff. The ability to recall something that was only briefly seen, having had little or no time to analyze, is more difficult to acquire.

The ABC's

When you were taught how to read and write, you first learned to recognise the shapes of each letter. You did this, in part, by drawing them over and over again. There is a difference, however, between learning one's letters and training one's visual memory. That difference is largely based upon the fact that you see letters and words throughout your life, on an almost constant basis. The act of simply existing in our modern world reinforces our memory of these symbols. This is not true for the observations which make up a drawing, painting or sculpture. These are seen, at best, over only a slightly-extended period.

The exact shape of an object, like a specific person's face, is not something we see nearly as frequently. In part this is because we and the person in question are in constant motion. My view of my wife's face at breakfast is different between the times when she picks up her coffee cup, when she's drinking and when she puts the cup back on the saucer. At which point am I seeing what could be defined as her shape? The answer is all of the positions and every one in-between. Your job therefore is to strengthen not only your ability to exactly remember the specific shapes that you only briefly see but also your ability to correctly and accurately perceive them.

Everything is Relative

Correctly determining the shape of something depends upon how the individual aspects of the shape relate to each other.* Even the simple definitions of geometric shapes depend on this fact. *A rectangle is composed of four straight sides connected by right angles with two of the parallel sides being shorter than the other two parallel sides.* That entire definition contains relationships. So, one of the ways to perceive a shape (as well as to remember it) is to think about it in terms of relationships.

Take a look at the image above. Which aspects of its contour are straight and which are curved? Think about how long those straight aspects are, relative to each other. How curved, relative to the straight sides, are the curves? How far apart are they? At what point are they the farthest apart? How about closest? These questions, and many others, are the types of things artists ask themselves almost continuously as they draw. At some point in their training, because they have asked themselves these questions so often, they are no longer always conscious that they are doing it. As related to memory drawing, these questions are integral and the quicker they become automatic for you the better.

Since you have already spent some time analyzing the shape, let's try to use it as your first memory drawing. There is no pressure since the shape is far more advanced than you are probably ready to manage at this point in your training. Lay a sheet of tracing paper

*How the object relates to any other object in the scene as well as to its visual environment are also considerations but they are outside the scope of this beginning lesson.

over the shape and trace the marked guideline. Then, close the book and attempt to draw the shape from memory. After your attempt, lay the tracing paper back onto the shape and compare it to the source image.

Lines, Lines and More Lines

Now that you've had a little taste of memory drawing, it is time to get down to the actual coursework. You will need a pad of tracing paper, a pencil (anything from a 2H to a 2B will do), a colored pencil, an eraser and a ruler. You will also need a clock or a kitchen timer. Feel free to photocopy the exercise pages and cut each shape out. In fact, when you begin a chapter it would be a good idea to do the same with the exercise pages.

The initial exercises which follow are composed of sets of straight lines followed by sets of straight and curved lines. The bottom line in each set will always be your guideline, and you will start by tracing that. You will memorize each set of lines at least twice. Your initial attempt at each set are meant to help improve your bottom-up memory abilities and the second time through your top-down abilities, in other words, seeing and knowing.

Using your ruler, trace the bottom line of set one and then put the tracing aside. Start the timer at three minutes and look at the original image while trying not to think about the length of the shorter line relative to the longer one. You are merely staring at the lines, not making any judgements about them. To that end, I find it helpful to occasionally focus slightly away from the lines and let them register in my peripheral vision. Focusing right in between them can help as well. After the timer goes off, put the source out of sight and try to draw shorter line next to the longer one you previously traced. Commence the drawing by marking the beginning and the end of the length of the line as you recall it and use your ruler to connect the dots. After drawing it stare into the middle and try to mentally compare what you have drawn with what you recall seeing and correct as necessary.

When you are confident in the dimension of your line, lay the tracing paper back over the source image to check your accuracy. Use the colored pencil over your drawing to trace out the correct line. If your memory drawing was exact, well done! If not, try the entire process again, only this time mentally compare the differences between the longer and shorter lines as you stare at them.

Alternate between these two methods until you can accurately reproduce the shorter line's length. Follow the same procedure for the other sets of lines on the next two pages and remember to strive for accuracy with each attempt. Naturally the curved lines will be more difficult to accurately recall but with time and practice your abilities will greatly improve. If, after doing all eight sets of lines you still have trouble being accurate on the second attempt, create your own sets and work on them until you consistently succeed.

Before you begin, read the chapter summary on page 69 for some hints on how to approach the exercises in this chapter.

1.

2.

3.

4.

Line Exercises

5.

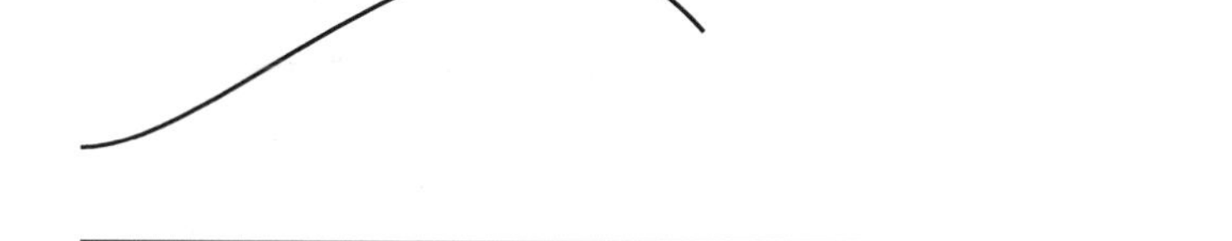

6.

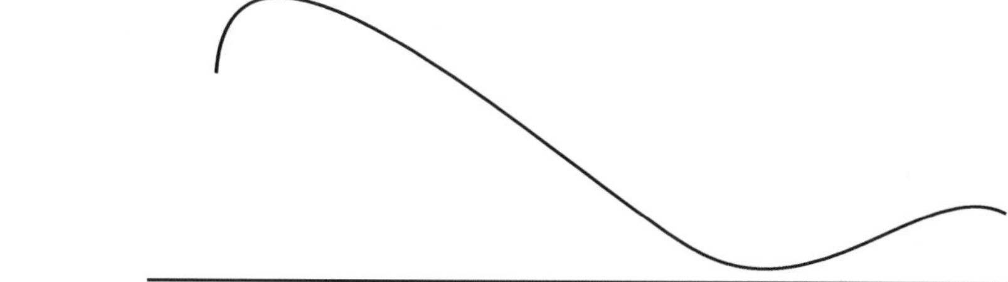

7.

8.

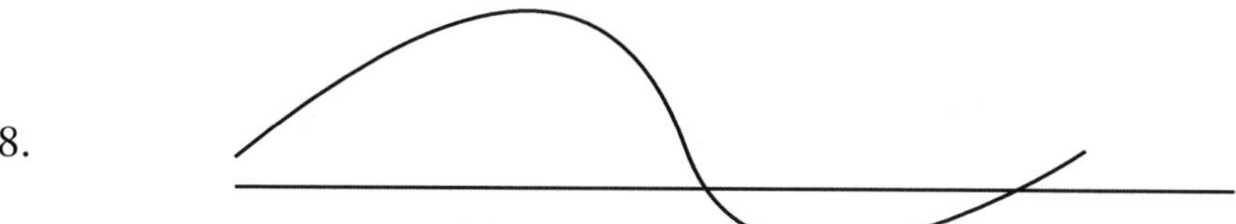

Line Exercises

Abstract Shapes

Notice that the shape which I had you recall near the beginning of this chapter was an abstract silhouette and also that it was greyed out. There are two reasons for this. One is that when using a more contrasted image, such as a black shape on a white background, our visual system sometimes creates a temporary afterimage. This is an optical illusion which, for a brief period of time after staring at the source, allows you to continue to *see* the image. That, of course, is not memory training. The limited contrast between the page and the grey shapes in the exercises is less likely to result in an afterimage.

The reason I created an abstract shape as opposed to a recognizable one is that I want to reduce the possibility that your mind could use its knowledge to help you recall the shape. As I mentioned before, your brain tends to want to recognize things, and it will use whatever recognizable shape it can to help with that. Here again, at least in the beginning stages of memory drawing, that is not memory training.

The shapes on the following two pages contain only straight lines. After those, the next two pages have shapes with curves in them.

Begin by tracing one side of the shape before you try to memorize it. Then look at the shapes for five minutes. On your first attempt for each shape simply stare into the center of the shape while you try to take it in as a whole. Then, follow the contour around with your eyes. During the session, occasionally trace the image in the air with your finger. You might also close your eyes now and then and try to form the image in your mind. On the second attempt, analyze its relational qualities as well. Make sure that you are far enough away from the shape that you can take the whole of it in without needing to scan around it with your eyes. Remember to check your accuracy after each attempt by tracing the shape on your drawing in colored pencil. If there was an error, do the same shape once again on the following day (or a couple of hours later) until you can do it perfectly.

If you find that you need more of these kinds of abstract shapes for additional exercises the best idea is to use some light grey construction paper and cut out random shapes with a pair of scissors. Cutting them out, as opposed to drawing them, will make it more difficult for your mind to recall their initial creation.

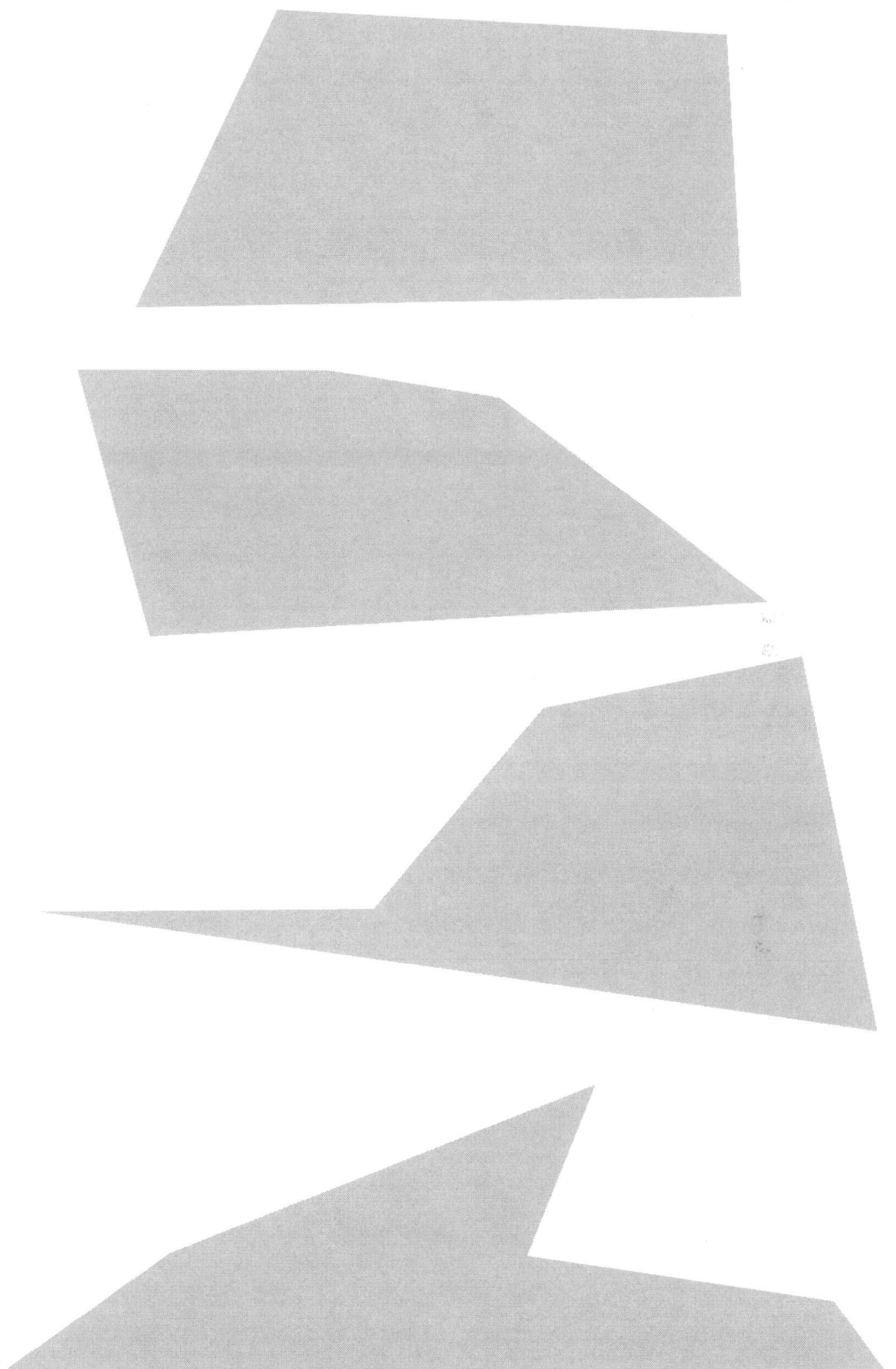

Abstract Shape Exercises

Abstract Shape Exercises

Abstract Curved-Shape Exercises

For these curved-shape exercises, do not trace any aspect of the shape. Stare at the shape for only three minutes instead of five minutes and do your best to simply observe them visually, without forming a mental word-thought.

Abstract Curved-Shape Exercises

Grecian Urn Forms

Historically, one of the ways taste was instilled into students was through the study of classical ornament and design. The artists who originally created these objects understood that part of artistic taste is the ability to discern when nature was to be reproduced as it is and when and how nature was to be adjusted. The student studying these objects learned that symmetry and proportion (which are aspects of how the parts relate to the whole; sometimes called the "big look") are components of a tasteful design. Many Grecian urns exhibit these characteristics and are therefore worthy of study.

The near symmetry of urn silhouettes is both a problem and a blessing. The problem is that you can become visually lazy when drawing them because your mind knows that one side of the shape is simply the mirror opposite of the other. But if you focus directly into the center of the shape while trying not to analyze it, you will begin to learn to perceive and remember the whole. When it comes to actually drawing the shape from memory, try to draw both sides of the image at the same time. In other words, don't finish one side and then copy, in reverse, the other.

On a sheet of tracing paper, trace the guideline I have given you (using the ruler to keep it straight) as well as the three marks. The guideline and marks will help you size the memory drawing accurately to the source and also give you a head start. Tape or tack the source up to a wall or an easel in front of you. You will then stand or sit around three feet away from it when trying to memorize. This will begin the process of learning to see and recall things which are not filling your field of view and help you learn to perceive shapes as a whole, in one glance.

Spend five minutes memorizing. On the first attempt do not analyze. Close one eye and stare into the center of the shape while you try to take it in as a whole. As with the previous abstract shape exercises, trace the image in the air with your finger. During the session, close your eyes now and then and try to form the image in your mind. You may then analyze on the second attempt if you like.

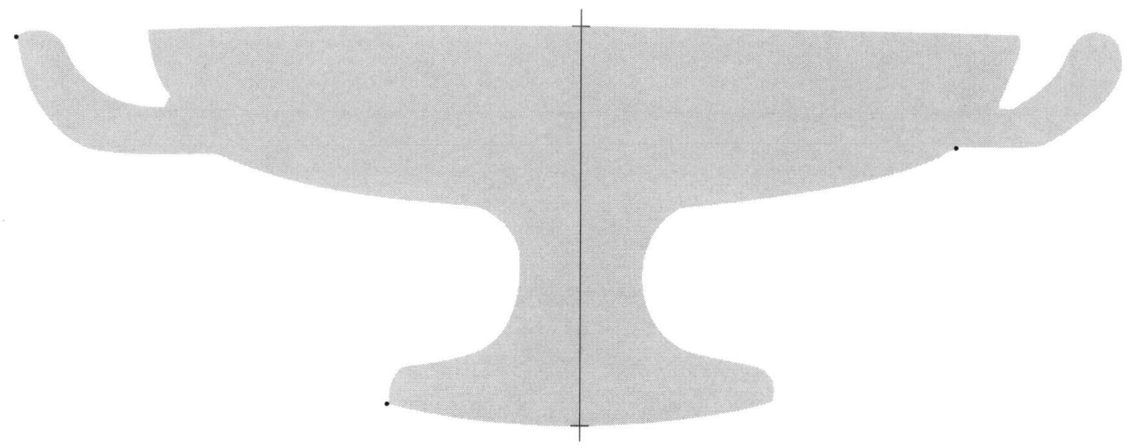

Grecian Urn Exercises

Grecian Urn Shape Exercises

Grecian Urn Shape Exercises

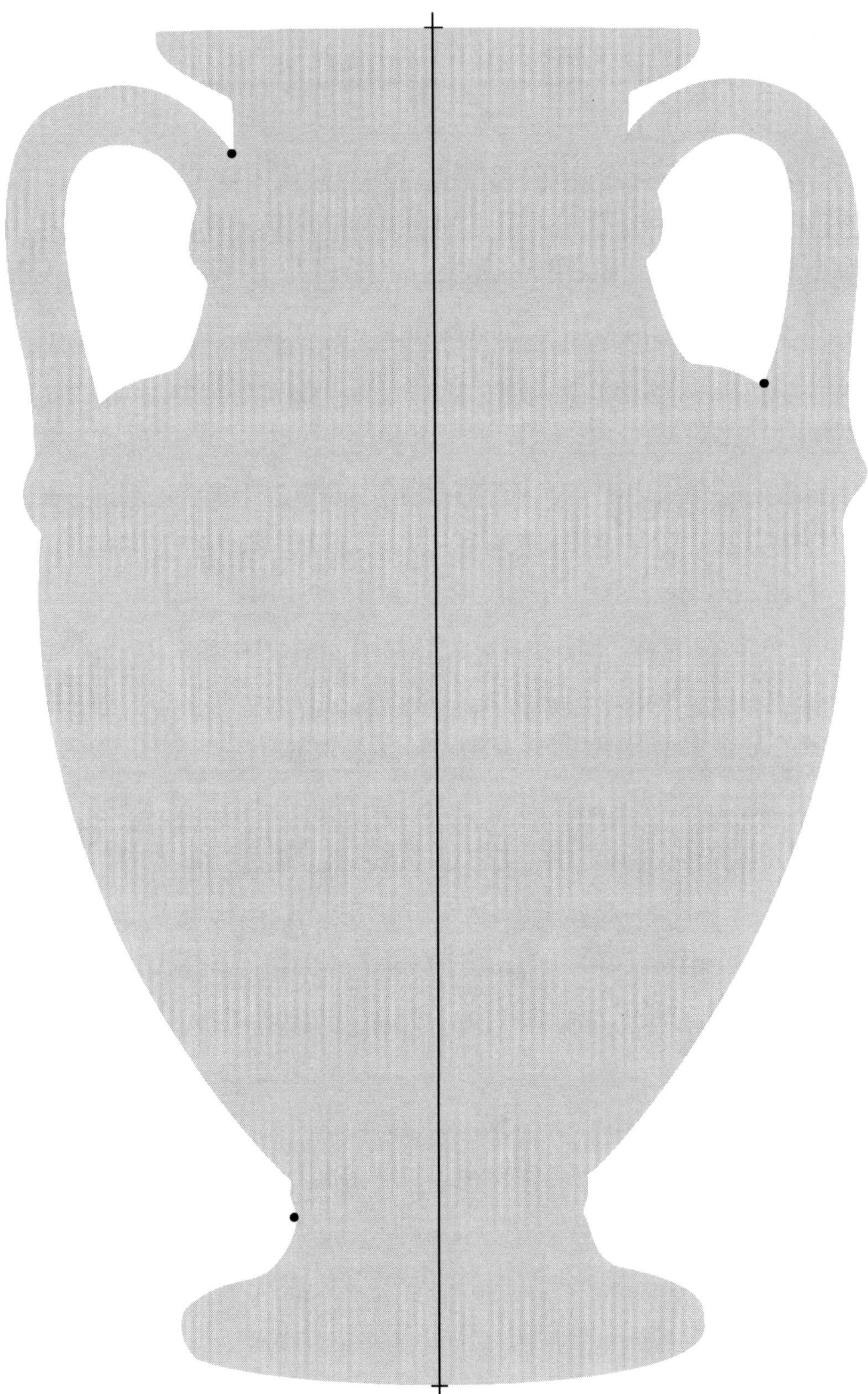

Grecian Urn Shape Exercises

Memory and Anatomy Training

Most representational art students will at some point need to learn anatomy. Interestingly, anatomical plates are oftentimes used as source images for memory training. The next four pages contain silhouettes of human bones, which I made from the plates of a classic anatomy book, *Artistic Anatomy* by Paul Richer, 1890 French edition. It is available in English as well, but any good anatomy book will do. Although I will only present a few of the images here, you would be wise to create your own after going through these exercises. If you do create the sources on your own, you could directly trace them, but my best advice is for you to draw them freehand as accurately as possible.

You are trying to permanently instill these anatomy images into your long-term memory, and therefore you should try to memorize them every so often. If you are diligent, you might consider these once-a-month exercises to be done over the course of a year or more.

Five to ten minutes is a good time frame for observing these anatomical images. Do each one, once per day, as many times as is necessary for your memory drawing to be consistently accurate. As before, try not to analyze the shape the first time or two when using each image. Rather, try to recall the non-verbal sight-impression.

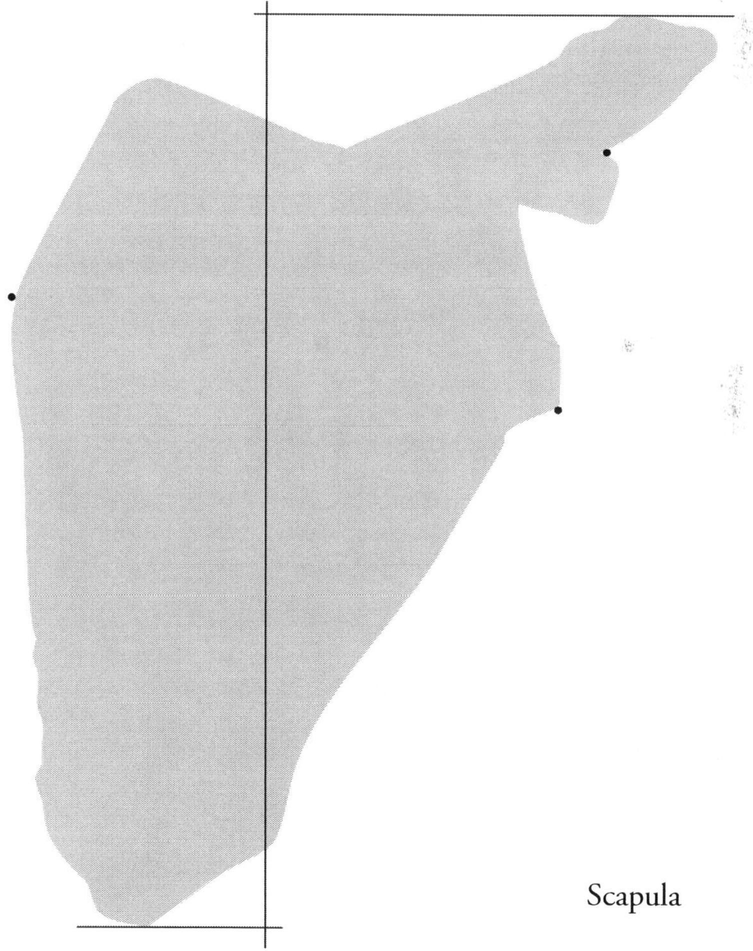

Scapula

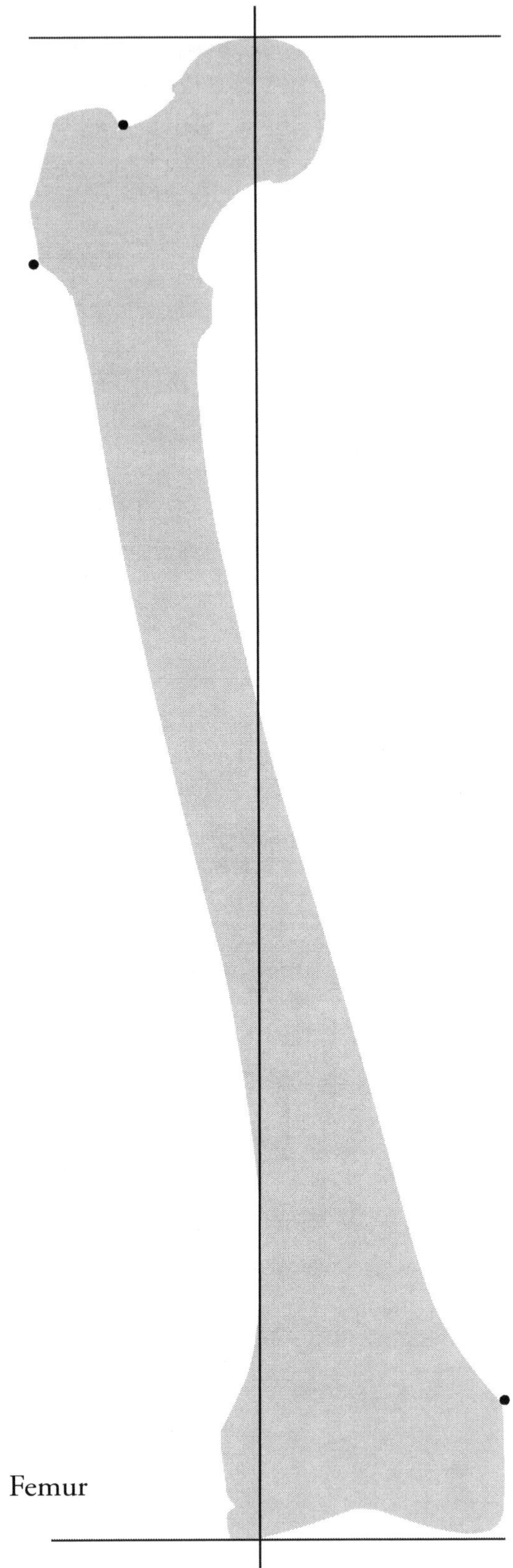

Bone Shape Exercises

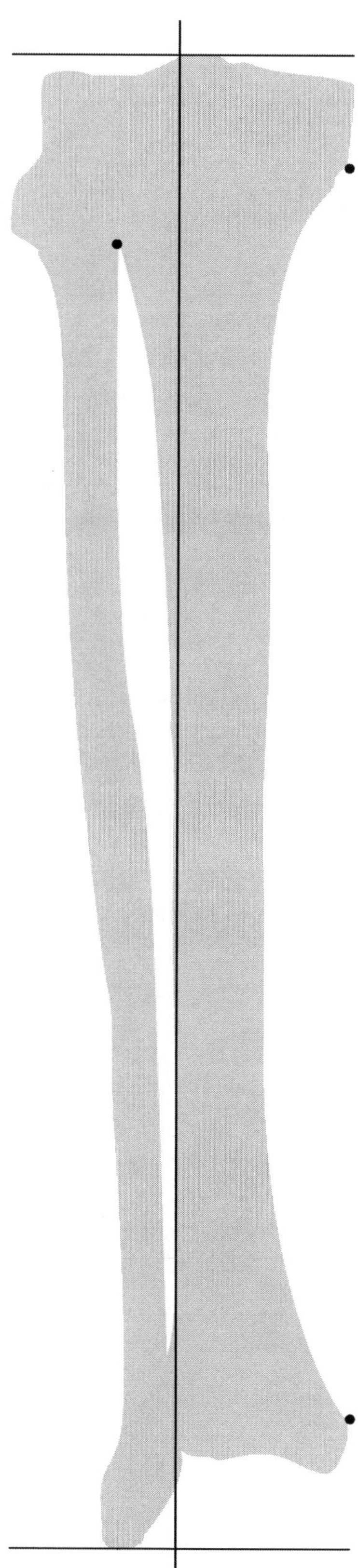

Fibula and Tibia

Bone Shape Exercises

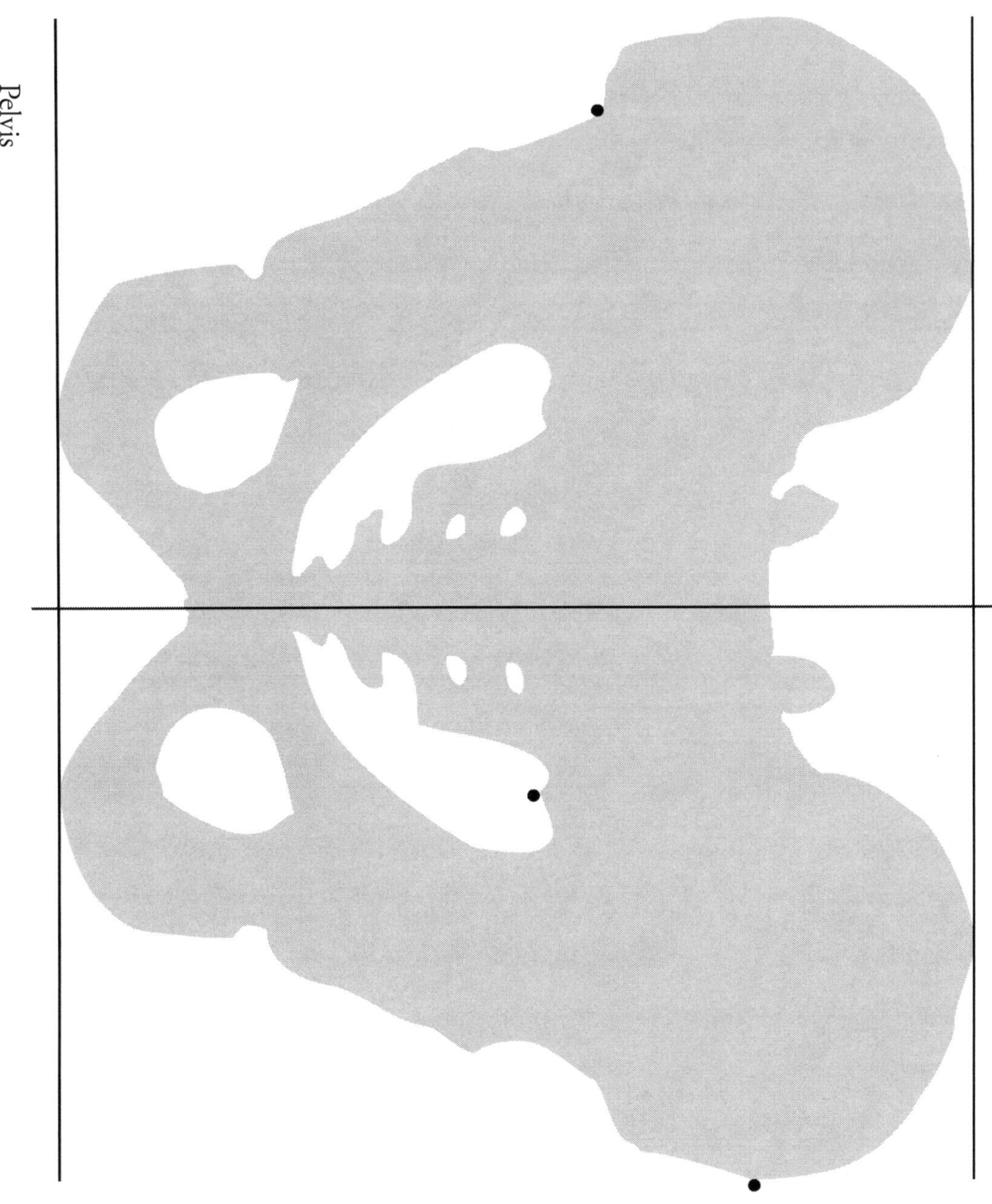

Bone Shape Exercises

Old Master Drawings

In the History chapter I mentioned that one reason for memory-drawing training was to increase your artistic storehouse of images. The anatomical plates in the previous exercise will have done that to a degree, but in more of a clinical fashion. For the *art* in artistic it is best to use Old Master drawings.

One of the ways a representational artist learns sound drawing technique is to copy fine drawings. In fact, back when apprenticeship was the principle form of art instruction, the apprentice spent a lot of time copying his master's drawings. These copies were often meant to be exact and as such they not only helped train the student to see but also to learn the master's technique. An additional benefit is that memorizing Old Master works will help you to develop your artistic sensibilities. For this reason you should always choose the best, most respected drawings and paintings. Using lesser artworks from minor masters will not only lessen that benefit, but it will put into your memory images which you may be better off not remembering. For our purposes, photographs are often in this category as well, so you should use them with caution. The *art* in photography is, while still visual, of a wholly different kind of art than the art in painting.

Rather than memorizing the sources I provide, you should draw them first. Before you begin though, read through Appendix IV for more information about making exact copies of Old Master drawings.

You will immediately notice that these are your first non-silhouette memory exercises. When drawing these from memory, feel free to incorporate whatever memories you have for the values which are present in them. However, at this point in your memory training, value is not your focus.

When doing these exercises follow the procedure below.
- Accurately copy the image first.
- When you are ready to begin your memory drawing, place a sheet of tracing paper over the source image (not your copy) and trace the plumb line, the top and bottom of the image and the reference points.
- Tack the source image to the wall or an easel and stand back a few feet.
- Set the timer for ten minutes.
- Stare at the source image, tracing it in the air with your finger now and then.
- The first time or two try not to analyze the image, simply absorb the abstract shape.
- When the timer goes off, put the source image out of sight and try to draw it from memory onto the prepared sheet of tracing paper.
- Check your memory drawing for accuracy by overlaying the source image.
- Using a colored pencil, trace out the correct lines wherever you made an error.
- Use the same source drawing, once per day, until you achieve an overall accurate result. Be aware that this may take a few days to a full week.
- You should cease using the reference marks on the source image as your accuracy improves.

Michelangelo, *Studies of a Seated Man*

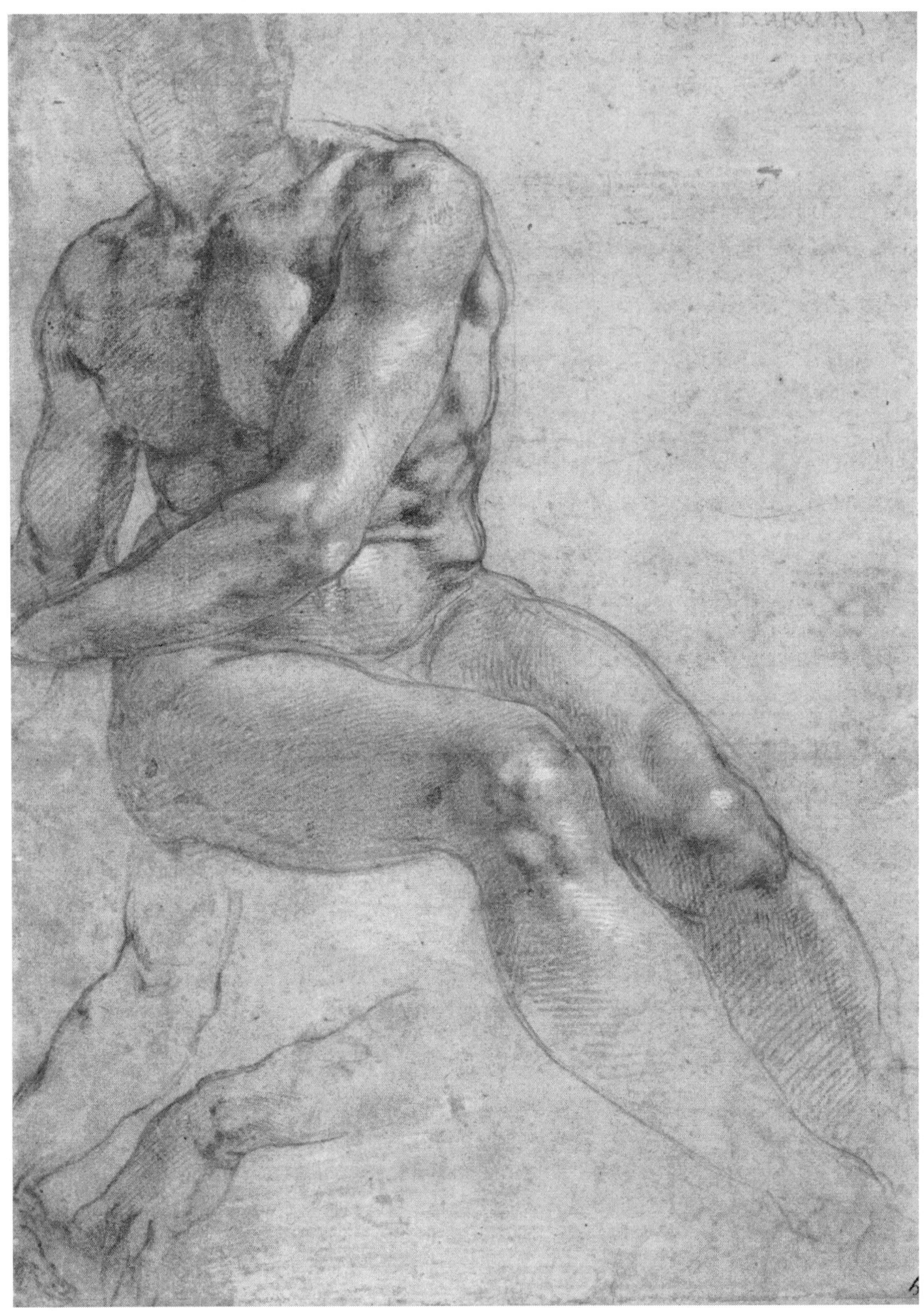

Old Master Figure Exercises

Raphael, *Kneeling Nude Woman*

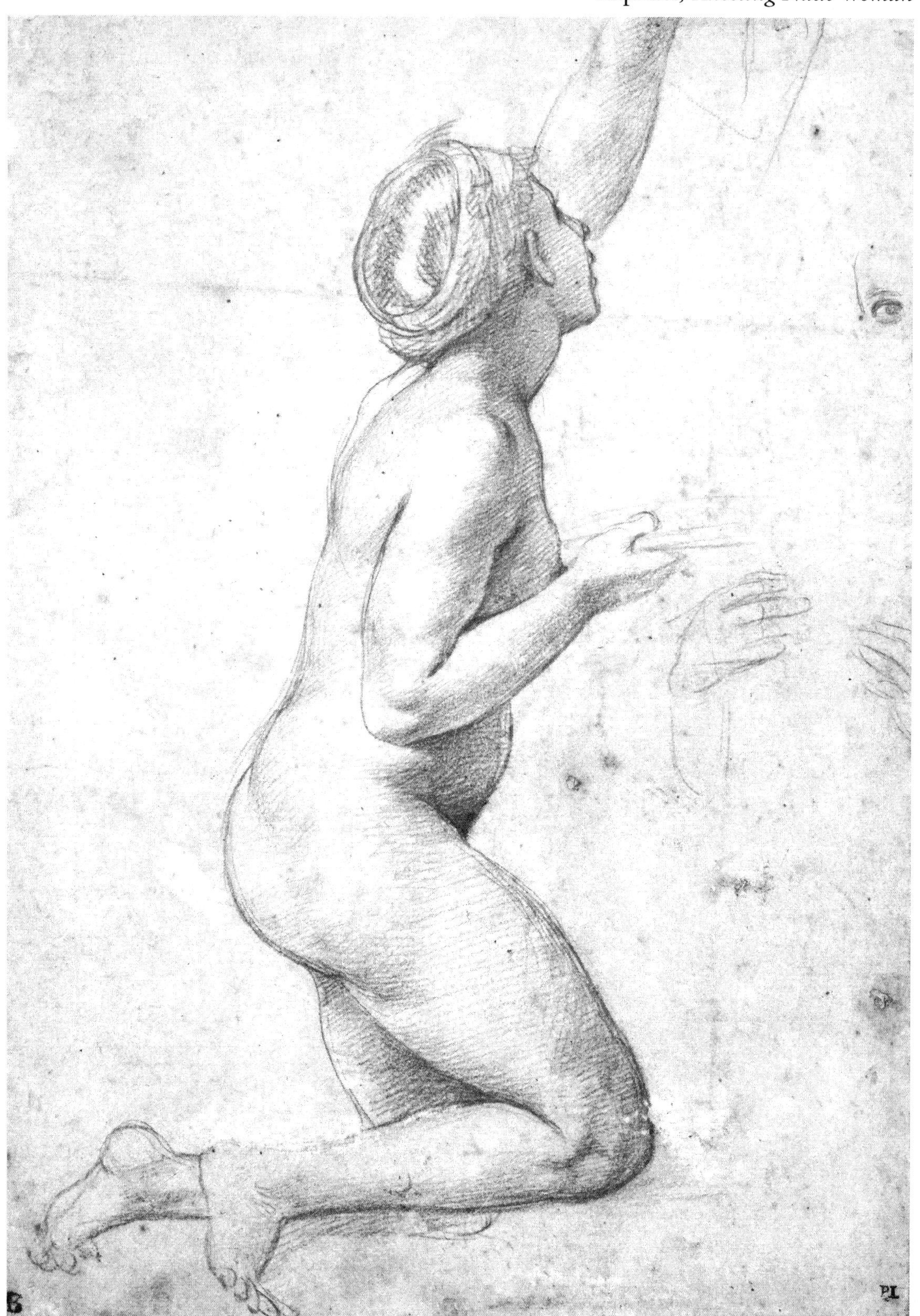

Old Master Figure Exercises

Rubens, *Studies of a Man Pulling*

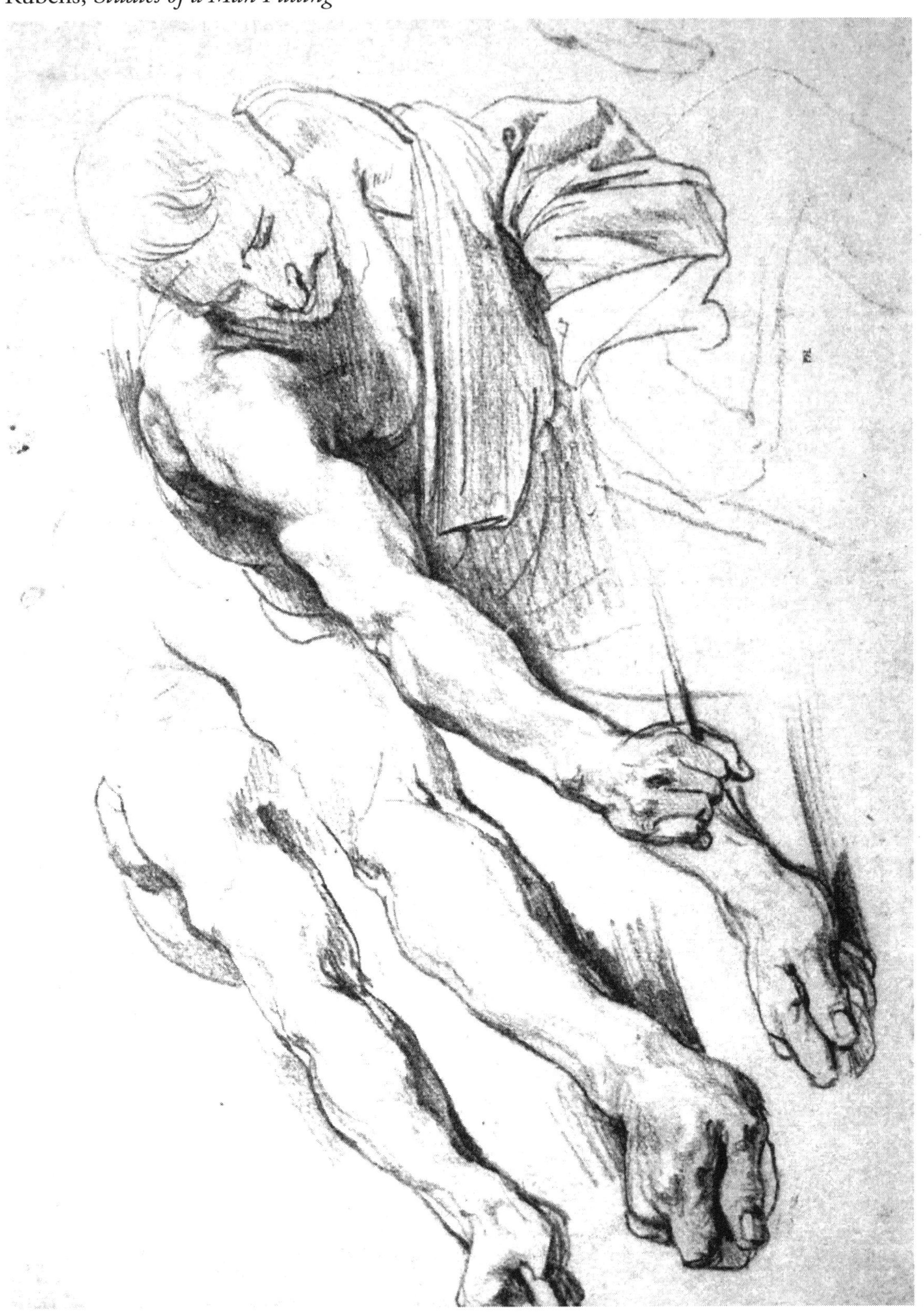

Old Master Figure Exercises

Prud'hon, *Woman Standing with a Broom*

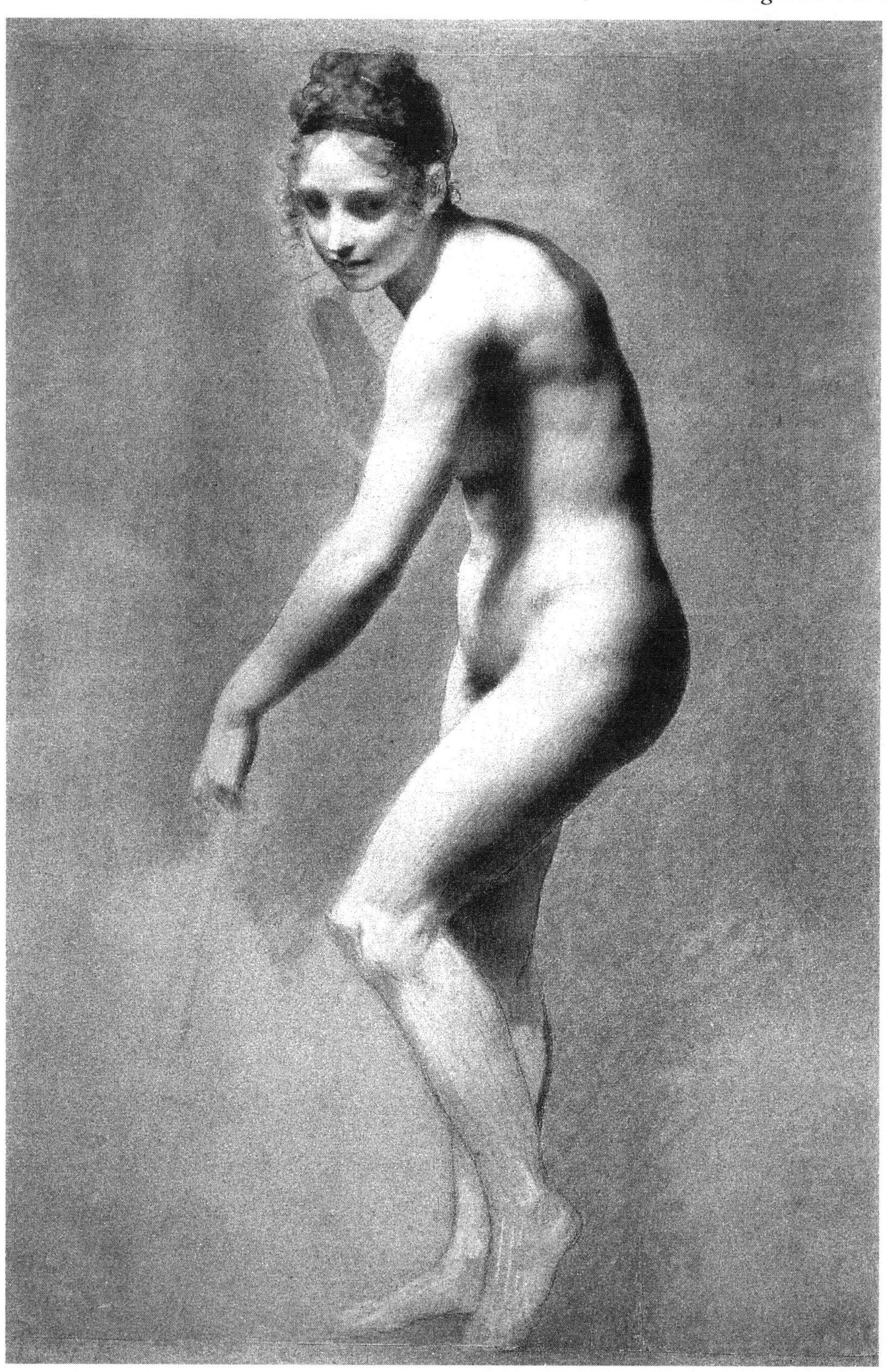

Old Master Figure Exercises

From the Round

Pre-flattened drawings are one thing, but life is three-dimensional. For the next set of shape exercises, you will need to use some simple objects. Vegetables, gourds, flowers pots or a jar would work. When I was in art school, I purchased a few plaster casts. One of them was of a human skull and I spent an entire summer memorizing it in different orientations.

Regardless of what your object is, place it about six feet away and in an environment where it is lit by only one light source. Use whatever drawing paper you prefer. You may find that dropping a plumb line is useful. If so, draw one on your paper as well. Stare at the object for ten minutes using the skills you have learned during the previous exercises. As these objects are not silhouettes, you will need to draw whatever interior aspects you might observe in them. Try to also observe, memorize and then draw the shadow line (also known as the *bedbug line* or *terminator*). Finish with a general shadow-tone.

After the time is up, cover the object or go into a different room and draw it from your memory. When finished, compare your drawing to the actual object. Using a dotted line or a colored pencil, redraw any errors you notice.

Memorize the same object, in the same orientation and lighting, everyday until you can accurately draw it from memory. Follow this routine for any number of objects until your speed and accuracy are good.

Evening Figures

If you are fortunate enough to be attending an atelier or regular figure-drawing sessions, now would be a good time to start memory drawings from the day's figure drawing. This should become a daily habit.

To do this properly, try to use the same method and materials as you did for the original figure drawing. Where I was trained, we would initially plumb the figure as well as establish where the top of the head and the bottom of the feet would be. You should do the same for the memory drawing, just like I have advised for the previous exercises. Try to do these as full images, not as silhouettes, and as such once you are confident with the entire contour, draw the bed-bug line as well. Finally, shade in the general shadow-tone.

I suggest that my students take two approaches to these drawings. One is to work on the same memory drawing in the evening for as many days as it takes to do the regular figure drawing. The other is to begin a new memory drawing of the same figure each evening. Alternating the approach with each new pose is a good routine to follow.

One of the benefits of this process is that you will begin to view the model in a way which prepares you for the memory drawing. This will push you into being more mindful of the ensemble - the whole - and will help to reinforce a complete perception of the figure.

Natural Forms

If you want additional study subjects, leaves and plants make great objects for memory drawing exercises, partly because they betray no mannerism in their design. For these, feel free to use any and all of the methods I have described to you so far.

Remember

- Every so often, reread the chapter on process.
- Focus your attention on the subject you are trying to memorize. Distractions and inattention are the biggest hindrances to memory.
- Close one eye.
- Rehearse the image, meaning, during the memorizing portion of the session, close your eyes now and then and try to form the image in your mind.
- Every so often physically trace the image in the air with your finger., then close your eyes and do it again.
- You might occasionally look away and try to draw it in the air a few times.
- When you are analyzing, begin with the large characteristics of the image and how they relate to each other, then move onto the smaller areas.
- Once you are consistently accurate in remembering the larger aspects of the shapes, begin chunking, which means grouping like-areas together in your mind.
- Verbally describe the shapes out loud.
- Review your attempts every week, and again every month, looking for errors which you consistently make. Learn from these mistakes by thinking about them during the future exercises. As an example, if you tend to make the shapes too wide, spend more time observing the width of the shapes and comparing them to the height.
- Every so often wait an hour or more between the end of the viewing time and when you do the memory drawing. During this wait period, go about your daily activities and at the same time think about the image you tried to memorize. After the wait period is over, try to draw the image as you normally would from your memory.
- Ongoing exercises may be found through a link on this website: http://www.memorydrawing.com.

·Value·

Although it is normal to commence a drawing with shape, form really begins to come into play when we add light and shade. Before progressing to the following value exercises, make certain that you have completed the exercises in the chapter on shape.

Squint and See the Forest

I teach my students to determine values by squinting when looking at their subject and their artwork. One of the reasons for this is that large areas of similar values in nature are often varied and squinting at them greatly simplifies or unifies those variations. Representing every little value-shift can lead to over-modeling and what is called, "looking into the shadows. Squinting helps mitigate these errors by allowing you to see the entire forest, not simply a bunch of unrelated trees.

Since the beginning exercises are already flat values, you may prefer to keep your eyes open normally. As the exercises become more complicated, you will better appreciate the value of squinting.

Relationships

The old adage that context is everything applies to correctly observing values. Although some artists do take a less relational approach in their work, our brain's perception of values is relative to their surroundings. With that in mind you will always do well to consider relationships when memory training.

The first time you attempt to memorize the exercises on the following pages, you are to use the left square as a guide. The second time through, try it without creating the reference square beforehand. You will then memorize the constant as well. Alternate in this way for each week's exercise.

Also notice that the area near the common edge of each square may appear to your eye as part of a gradient. This is an optical illusion and while you do not necessarily try to paint it that way, it should appear as such in your memory drawing.

Most of the following exercises should be done in your medium of choice. Bear in mind that the range, or gamut, the medium is capable of achieving will partially determine how successful you will be. The darker aspects of the source image may prove the most difficult to hit, and therefore I suggest that oil paint be used for the squares. This is because the gamut for oil paint is larger than for most other mediums. That said, pencil, charcoal, watercolor or acrylic will work if you prefer as what you are really training is your memory for value relationships rather than for the isolated values themselves.

- Draw the squares onto paper, canvas, canvas board or prepared paper. Shellacked, heavyweight paper works well.
- Place the source squares on the wall or an easel, three to four feet away.
- Alternate using the left reference square as a constant with memorizing it.
- For the paired values, set the timer for three minutes. Set it for five minutes for the multiple-value squares.
- As your memory for values improves, try to drop back to three minutes regardless of how many squares you are memorizing.
- Stare at the source image, comparing its value to the reference square. When the timer goes off, put the source image out of sight and try to draw or paint it from memory onto the prepared sheet.
- To check your memory drawing for accuracy, place it next to the source image and stand back. Then, flick your eye between the source and your painting. You should also squint down to see if your drawing and the source appear to blend together.
- Do the same pair or multiple-value squares, once per day, until you achieve an accurate result.
- When you complete the exercises from this section, cut out squares of greyscale construction paper (of different values) and use them as your sources.
- Continue these pairs and multiples until are able to be consistently accurate.

The source image

The memory drawing

In the example above, the source image on the left - has two shaded squares and the memory drawing, on the right, has the left square already shaded in. I call the left square, "the constant." You are to memorize the value of the right square, relative to the constant. To do this however, means that you will first need to create the constant.

Instead of actually drawing or painting the constant, when the time comes to paint from your memory you could simply use the square itself by placing it next to the square you are trying to paint.

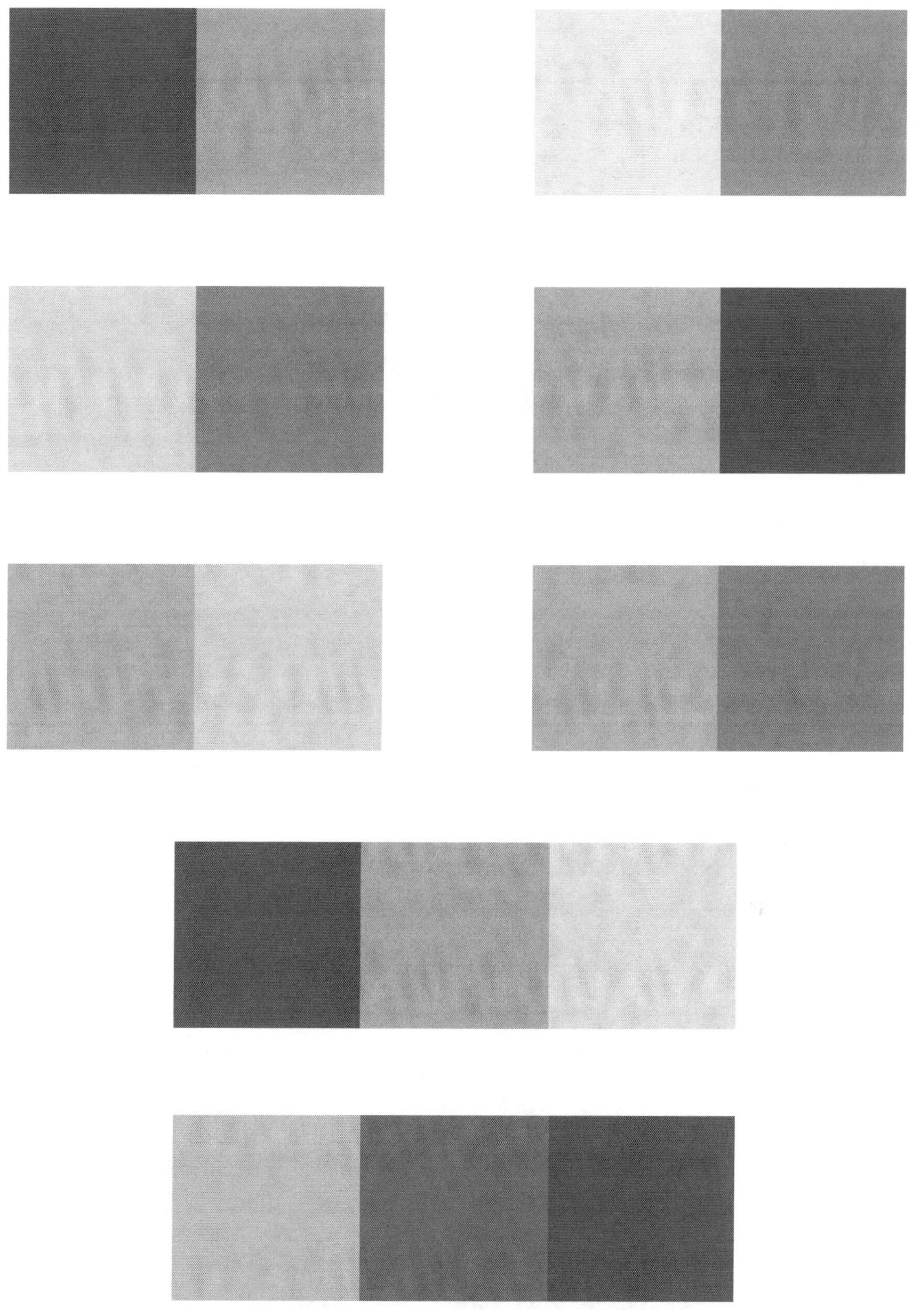

Paired and Multiple-Value Exercises

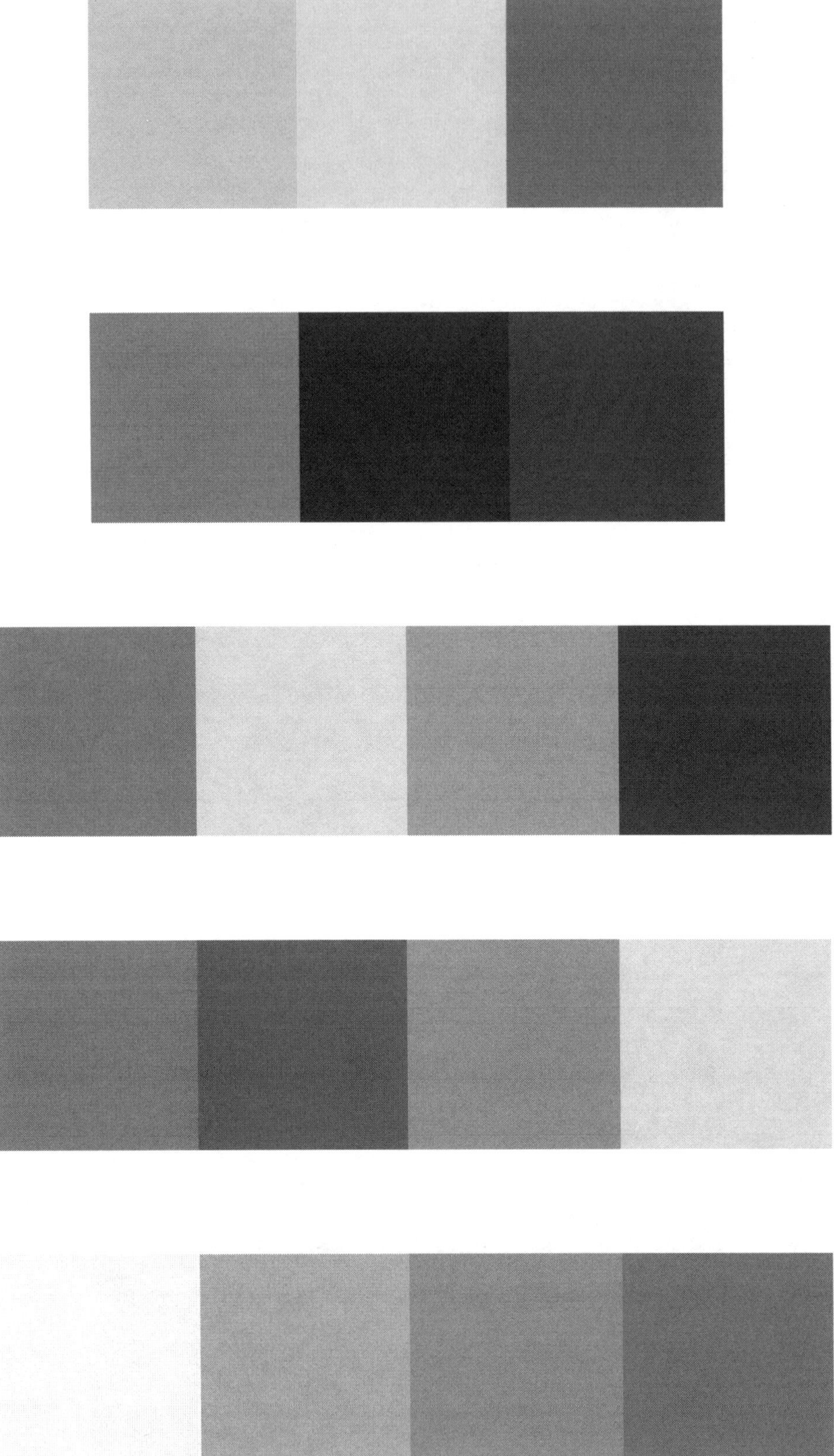

Multiple-Value Exercises

Memory for Edges

Memorizing edges is not something that is traditionally done when memory training. I believe that one reason for this is that when recalling a scene, edge is often reduced to a formula. In other words, the artist softens or sharpens the edges in the scene based upon their foreknowledge of its characteristics rather than an actual, recalled observation of them. Given the limited amount of time the artist usually has to observe the intended object or scene, this is hardly surprising. An additional issue is that edges in nature are infinitely varied. These variances are not just edge to edge but within each edge itself. This means that a single edge will likely vary between softer and sharper areas all along its path. Obviously this complicates things.

I do not consider edge memory training as important as shape, value and color-memory training. Nonetheless, some attention should be paid to it as edges are as much a part of our visual field as the other aspects. As your memory for value improves, more complicated sources will require that you have some awareness of edge relationships.

What is an Edge?

Every value change, if discernible at all, has an edge. How sharp or soft that value transition appears to be is dependent on the abruptness of the value change. This abruptness is affected by a number of things like the distance of the light source to the object or how physically sharp or soft the tactile edge of the form actually is. When the edge is not on the contour of an object it is variously called the "bed-bug" line or the "terminator." Regardless of the reason for the edge or its term, your initial task is to observe where that edge is. After that observation, the next step is to determine how wide the gradient is. The softer the edge, the wider the gradient. The sharper the edge, the narrower the gradient.

Edges in Context

In keeping with the main organization of the course, I suggest that students begin with edges which are observed independent of an object or scene. The edges still need a context however, because merely saying that something is sharp is almost meaningless outside of its context. With that in mind, as with value perception, proper edge perception begins with correctly observing relationships. This is part of analysis, of course, but it is also a part of perception. As before, you are training yourself to recall those perceptions as much as to recall your analysis of them.

Analysis requires that you actively categorize the many different visual aspects of your subject. This is equally important when doing regular drawing and painting exercises as when memory training. As you progress in your studies, searching out the darkest darks and lightest lights becomes an unconscious habit, as does discerning the sharpest sharp edges and softest soft edges.

Sources

Sourcing edge examples to use for exercises is in some ways a bit of a challenge. One idea is to set up a lamp or a spotlight and direct it at a simple object like a can or a coffee cup. Put a sheet of white paper under the object so the cast shadow edge is clearly seen. Make sure to place the light close enough to the object so that it casts a long shadow on the paper. Using two pieces of black tape, section off a portion of the cast shadow's edge which includes some edge variation. Besides defining the boundary of your study area, the tape provides a sharper, contrasting edge for you to compare to the shadow edge.

On a sheet of paper use a 2B pencil and a ruler to draw a rectangle that is large enough to contain the taped off section of cast shadow. Within the rectangle, try to accurately copy the value of the light and dark as observed on either side of the edge. - Do not press too hard on the pencil, however, as you may be lightly erasing to create the edge when you do the actual exercise. Bring these values directly together, creating a sharply defined edge, but make sure that the resulting edge is different than the actual edge you see on your source. This process creates the values on each side of the edge, in other words, your constant.

Now, try to memorize this section of your source over the course of three minutes. The first time through, simply observe the edge in its entirety, relative to the sharpness of the edge of the tape. Pay attention to the whole area around the edge, not just the transitional edge in question. It may help to look slightly away from the area as you can then more effectively take in the whole of the edge and the values which created it. After the time is up, move away from the source and attempt to blend the edge on your paper to the level you recall seeing it on the source. If you use a blender (also called a tortillion or blending stick) in your regular classes, use one for these exercises as well. If not, then do not try one here. Avoid using your finger as, at least in this case, it is too blunt of an instrument. Once you finish, lay your drawing right next to the source, positioned in a way that it is completely within the light. Flick your eye between it and the source. An accurate drawing will show no difference between the two.

On the next attempt using the same subject, you may analyze while observing. When analyzing, compare the soft edge to the sharpness of the tape edges. Here again three minutes would be a good time frame.

For other exercises, changing the level of sharpness on the source is as simple as adjusting the light's position relative to the can. Do a number of these exercises until you can successfully memorize edges when using the constant. You should then begin to do the entire process from memory, values and edge, without creating the constant beforehand.

- Make sure that you are consistently accurate in your value-square memory exercises before you attempt edge memory exercises.
- Even though these exercises involve values, I recommend beginning with pencil or charcoal. As your recall skill increases, feel free to use paint.
- Spend only three minutes of observation time for each exercise session.

Memory Cast Drawing

Drawing from antique sculpture or plaster casts has been a tradition in representational arts education for centuries. Since its benefits are well known, I will not elaborate on them here. What is less well known is that casts are as useful for memory drawing.

Real objects present a number of challenges for memory drawing beyond those which are seen in flat sources. In addition to the difficulty of accurately checking your results, the main concern is depth. As in regular drawing, depth is conveniently dealt with by closing one eye. This process flattens the image and you may even already be doing it in your daily art classes. Clearly, the images in this book are flat, but you may still find it helpful to close one eye when doing the exercises. When you progress to real objects, you should continue to close one eye when observing.

The process of memorizing real-world objects is a mixture of everything you have learned up to this point. For the initial attempt each day, you should try not to analyze too often. Instead, take the image in as a whole. This means, observe the shapes, values and edges together as a complete unit. Keep in mind that you should not expect to do very well at first. Unlike the previous exercises, you will work on the same drawing over a number of days. Nonetheless you should try to capture the entirety of the image in this drawing, not merely a part of it. The errors you make on this first attempt will help guide you during the next session. Pay special attention to these as one of the tenets of mastery is to focus on correcting errors.

On the second attempt, which is the analysis stage, try to perceptually alternate between shape and value as you stare at the object. In other words, alternately think about the shapes and then the values. When analyzing you will be tempted to rely on your knowledge of how light and shade function. In the real world this is fine and even necessary. However, your memory will become more well-trained if you fight against this during the exercises. It is not unlike using a calculator. Using one when balancing your checkbook is common-place and even a time saver, but it is cheating when taking most math tests.

As noted in the previous section, edge relationships play a central role in representing the illusion of depth. Here again you will be tempted to rely on your knowledge-base of how light and shade works, but you will be better served to try to forget that for a time. To begin, you will try to memorize a flat mosaic of light and dark shapes which, when correctly realized, look like a simplified version of the rounded source image.

When you get to the point where your memory drawings and paintings are accurate in shape and value you can also attempt to observe edge relationships and memorize them.

Beginning With Bargue

The drawing on the following page originated in a book of lithographic prints which was called the *Cours de Dessin*. Charles Bargue collaborated with Jean-Léon Gérôme to produce the course in the late 1860's. At present, a modern-day edition of the course is available through most bookstores and it is in use by ateliers worldwide. Numerous versions of the plates are available online, for free, as well.

I have my doubts about teaching adults how to draw through flat copy work, but there are some advantages to it. However, at this stage in your memory-drawing training, Bargue-Gérôme plates make great sources. They can certainly help to teach the student how to simplify what they observe.

Notice that the image below shows the beginning and the finished version of the cast. Also notice that the beginning stage is blocked-in with facets. I recommend this approach to beginning a drawing but I am aware that many do not. See Appendix III for a discussion of both sides of this issue.

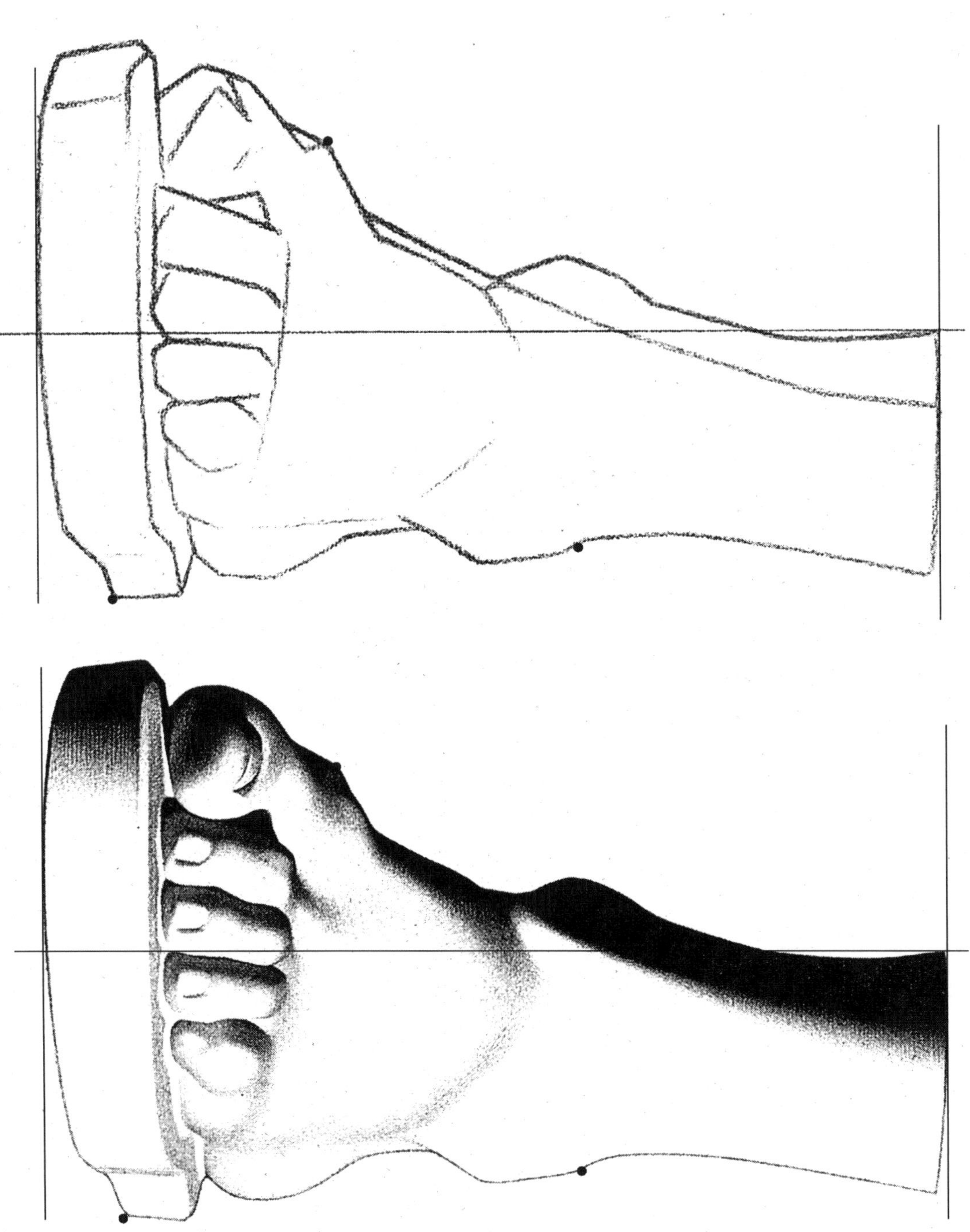

Cast Memory Exercises -A plate from Bargue's *Cours de Dessin*

Regardless of whether you prefer to use facets or curves, cast memory exercises from the flat, as well as three-dimensional objects should commence in a simplified fashion, similar to the left-hand image on the previous page.

If you have been quite accurate up until now, use the finished drawing on the right as your memory source for this first exercise. If you are still struggling with accurate shapes, use the left-hand image. If that is the case, you might consider holding off on the following exercises until your accuracy improves.

In addition to memorizing the contour, special attention should be given to the bedbug line. This line defines the main breakpoint between light and shade and as such it is very important to our perception of depth.

Before commencing with the photographs on the following pages and real-world objects, do your best using the plate of the foot on the previous page. It would be wise to do a few additional plates from the *Cours de Dessin* book as well and you may find some examples in the weekly exercises section through a link on this website:
http://www.memorydrawing.com

Follow the instructions below when memory-drawing from Bargue-Gérôme plates and from the cast photographs on the following pages. They are sound principles to follow when you graduate to three-dimensional sources as well.

- Make sure that you are able to accurately recall the shape and value exercises on the previous pages before you attempt cast or real-world object exercises.
- Even though these exercises involve values, I recommend beginning with pencil or charcoal. As your skill increases feel free to use paint.
- Spend around ten minutes observation time for each exercise session.
- In the beginning, work on the same drawing for three days. Once you can succeed fairly accurately in the third session, drop to two sessions per drawing.
- When you can accurately recall the images in this section, use three-dimensional objects or even purchase your own cast.
- White or off-white vases work as well, as do coffee cups.
- When observing values, begin by searching for the darkest darks and lightest lights.
- Look for the larger value patterns .
- When observing edges, begin with the extremes: sharpest sharp and softest soft.
- Every so often wait an hour or more between the end of the viewing time and when you do the memory drawing. During this period, go about your daily activities, thinking about the image you tried to memorize. After the period is over, try to draw the image as you normally would from your memory.

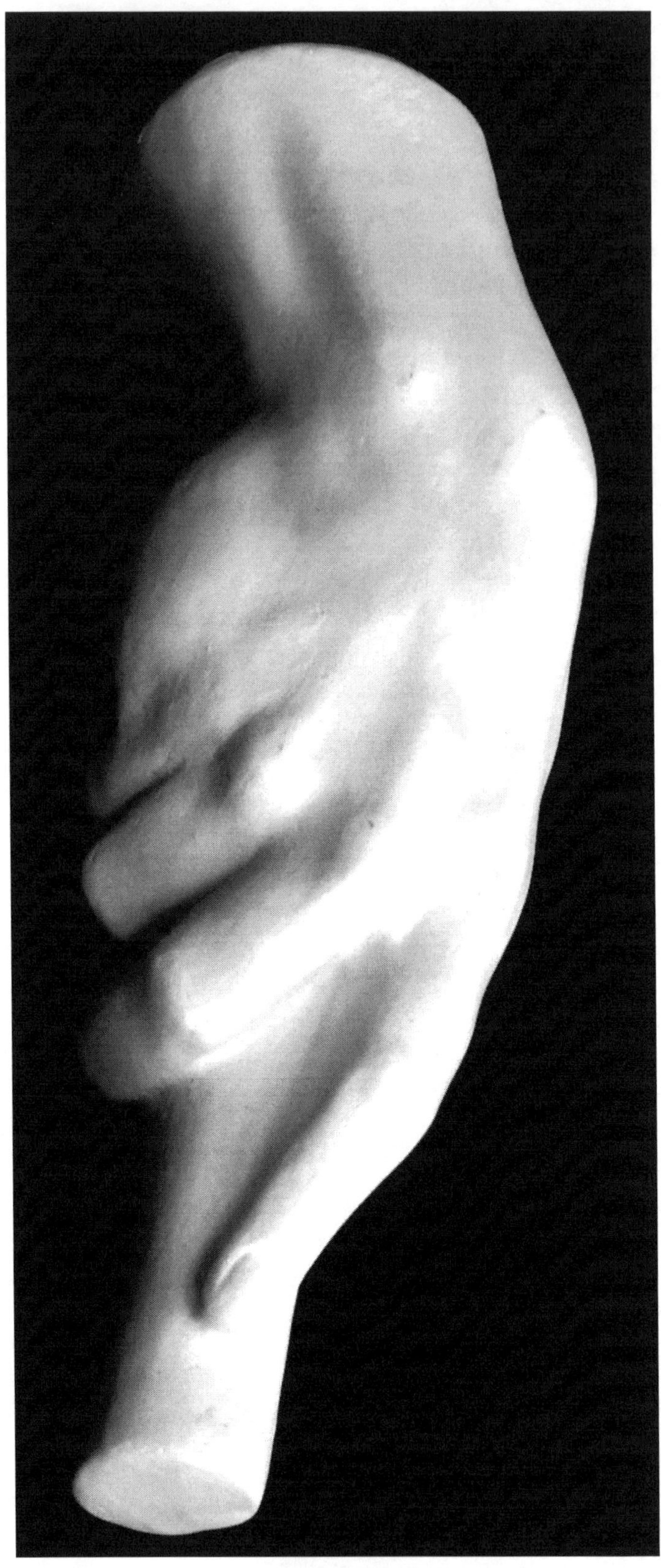

Cast Memory Exercises

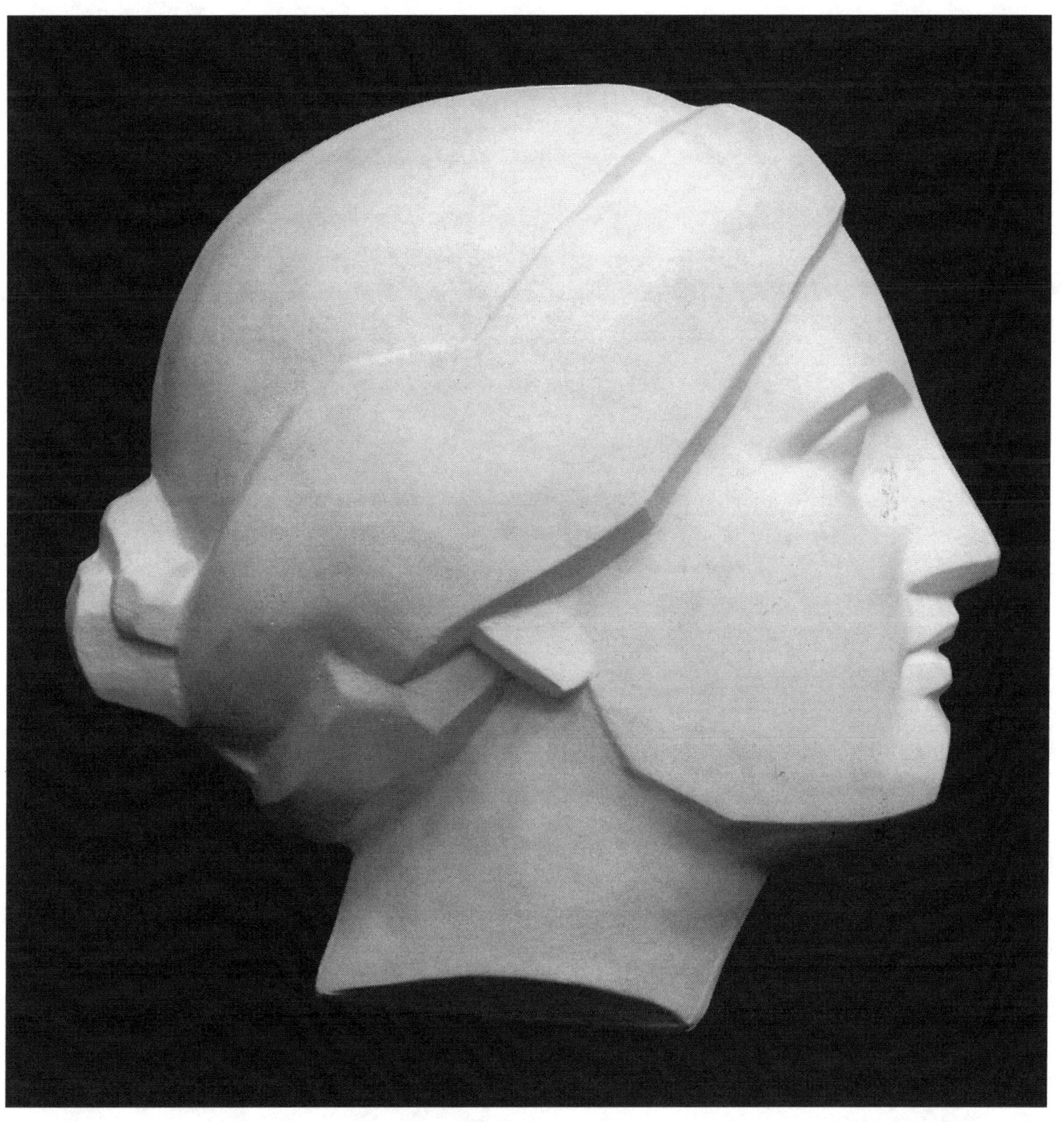

Cast Memory Exercises

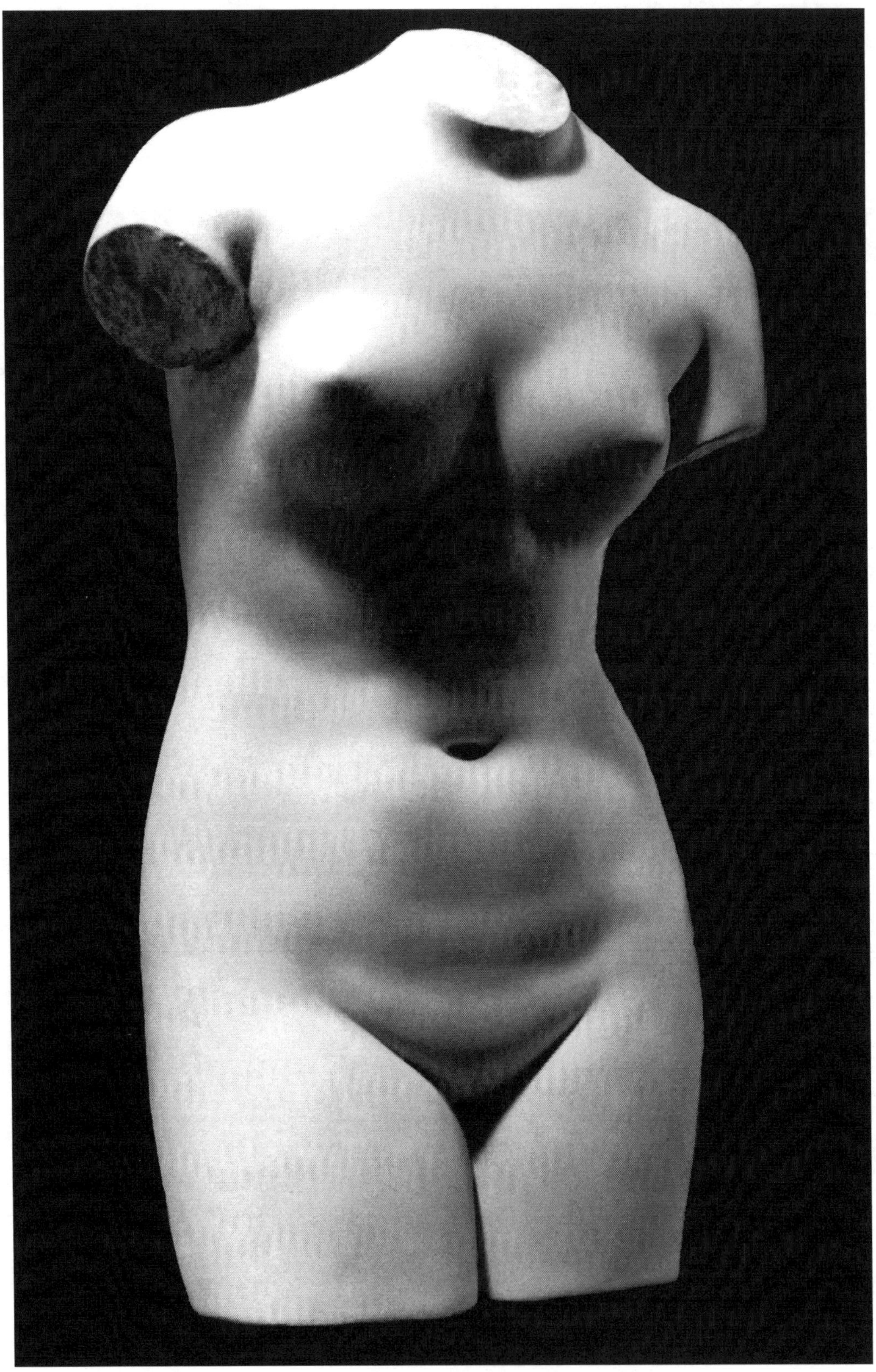

Cast Memory Exercises

Memory for Scenes

All of your hard work so far has led to this section for it incorporates shape, value and edge as presented in a scene. Eventually you will use actual scenes, but to begin with I, like Boisbaudran before me, suggest using Old Master paintings for your exercises. A further advantage is that it will help you learn composition.

Our brains have a remarkable capacity to recall scenes. Try to picture any place you have been and you will quickly see what I mean. But that memory is most often generalized. Just how much information is remembered and how accurately that information is recalled is really the subject in question. Earlier I mentioned that accurate visual memory is an active, intentional process and that it begins with perception. Your memories of the places you have been were likely remembered because of experience, not because they were intentionally observed. As helpful as experience is for memory, viewing a scene with purpose is far more helpful for accurate recall later on.

Success in this endeavor depends in large part on seeing the whole of the scene. Don't fret though as we seem to be hard-wired to do just that. Many cognitive psychologists believe that the primary way we recognize objects, faces and scenes is holistically (which again, is a more scientific term for the "big look"). It is not the color of my eyes that causes you to recognize me, rather, it is the overall shape of my face along with how my features relate to it and to each other.

Unfortunately, the act of traditional drawing can shift our brains out of perceiving holistically into more of a piecemeal approach. This is because when we draw, we naturally tend to focus in on the part being drawn instead of the part's relationship to the whole. Many successful artists even prefer this way of drawing and this book is not necessarily meant to change that. However, piecemeal seeing will get you nowhere fast when it comes to memory drawing because when you only fixate on a part, you tend to lose the whole.

Sketching, Gesture Drawing and Memory Drawing

Drawing scenes or figures from memory eventually brings up the idea of sketching. Unlike finished drawing, sketching is something which tends to force most students into a kind of holistic seeing. If you look around at the participants in any short-pose figure sketch group, you will notice that most are drawing the whole figure and a few are only drawing a detail of it. Those who are drawing the whole figure are likely doing something called, *gesture drawing*. Their goal is to represent the essential movement, or gesture of the pose, quickly, because the pose only lasts for a brief period of time. In order to succeed, the artist needs to view the figure, or scene, holistically - as a whole.

However, gesture drawing tends to rely at some point on construction (using stick-figures, ovoids, cylinders or block-forms) or overly sketchy lines, most of which bear little direct relation to the actual forms being observed. They are lines in search of a form. This, of course, is not memory drawing.

Due to the way I was trained, I am not completely sold on gesture drawing as a course of study. It can lead to sloppy execution in long-pose drawing, and in extreme cases, sloppy seeing overall. Nonetheless there can be some benefit to it. If the student can learn to seize the essentials of the pose or scene and keep the awareness of the whole in mind when they are working on longer poses, then the exercise will have achieved its purpose.

This admonition also applies to memorizing shape, value and scene observations. As Leonardo correctly observed, it is the whole of the image that is important, not merely the unrelated parts.

> *When you draw a nude, sketch the whole figure and nicely fit the members to it*
> *and to each other. Even though you may only finish one portion of the drawing,*
> *just make certain that all the parts hang together, so that the study will be useful*
> *to you in the future.* -Leonardo da Vinci

Old Master Memory Sketches

Memory drawing and memory sketching are really the same thing. I make the distinction only because the term *sketching* seems to result in the student feeling less pressure to perform. Furthermore, a sketch is normally considered part of a process rather than an end result. Keep this in mind when doing the rest of the exercises in this chapter.

Making small, thumbnail sketches of paintings which you admire is a great help in learning composition. These sketches should represent the main shapes in the painting in terms of simple value patterns. In his book on composition, Henry Poore states that, *"Every picture is a collection of units or items and every unit has a given value."*[1] Sketching scenes from memory is doing just that, delineating the large patterns of discrete value.

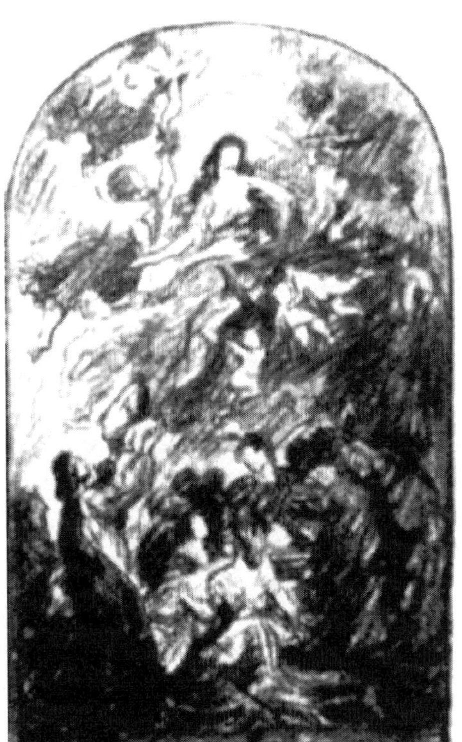
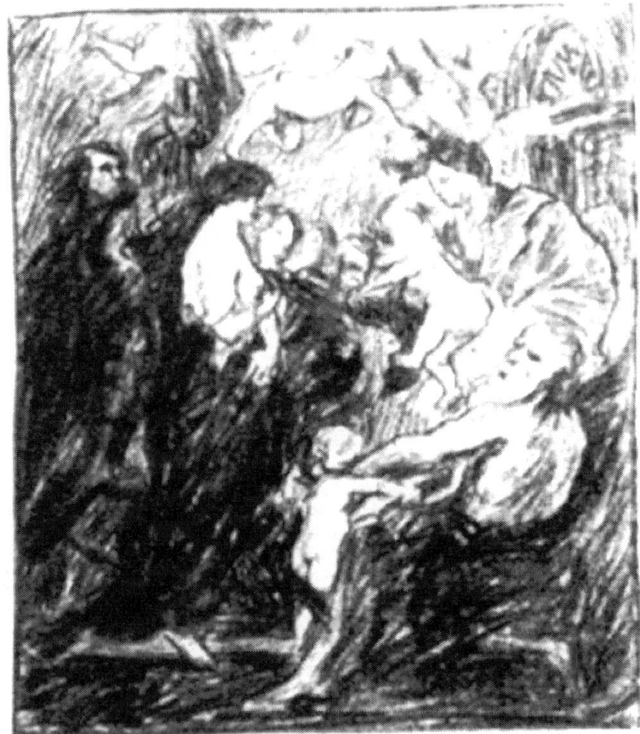

Sketches from Rubens[2]

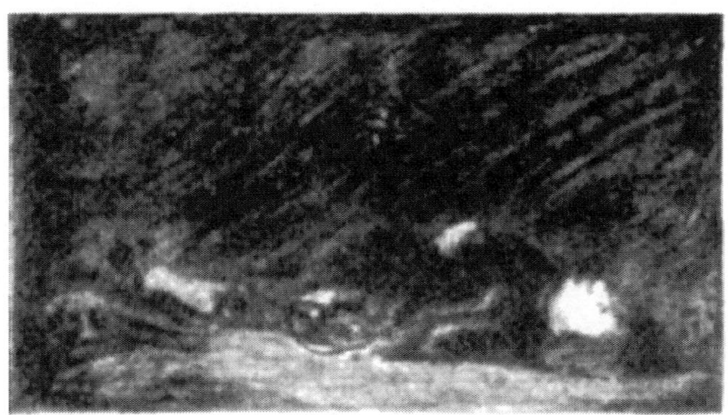
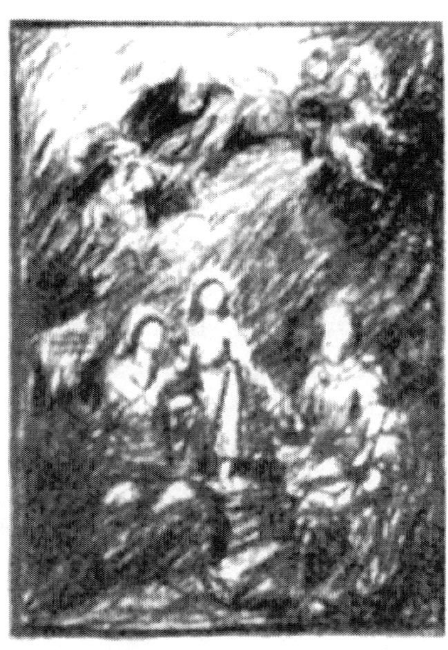
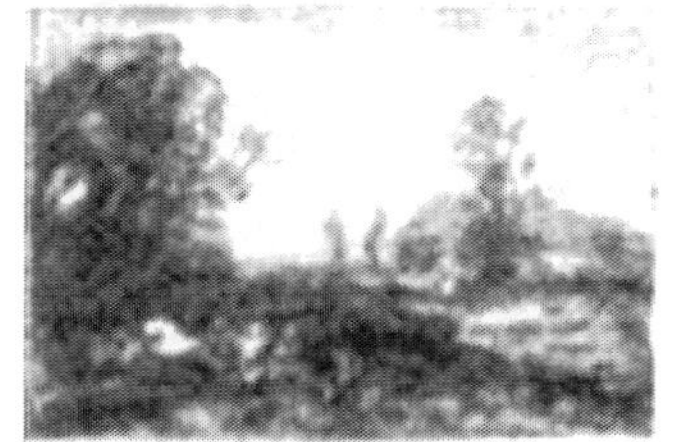
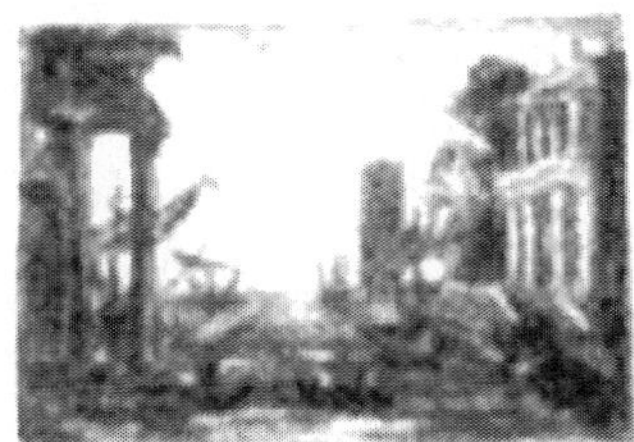

Sketches from Manet, Lorrain and Murillo[3]

The images above and on the previous page are from Poore's book, *Pictorial Composition and the Critical Judgement of Pictures*, and they are fine examples of thumbnail sketches from Old Master paintings. Although he did them while viewing the actual paintings, the result is similar to what a memory sketch should look like.

These sketches can be done after viewing the image of the painting in an art book or on a computer screen as well as after having seen the painting in person. If you live near a museum with fine Old Master paintings, so much the better. When at the museum, spend about ten minutes looking. After that, go into another room, outside or into the museum's cafeteria and do your best to sketch it into your sketchbook with a pencil or pen. When you have finished, make sure to go back to the painting in order to check your accuracy.

If you are viewing a reproduction at home, you would be better off using charcoal and white chalk on mid-tone grey charcoal paper than pencil or pen. Having those three, given values will help you to remember value patterns. Follow the same procedure as above: spend ten minutes observing, create the memory sketch and then check your work.

Scene Impressions and Analysis

After succeeding with at least a dozen Old Master memory sketches, it is time to try your hand at actual scenes. Although the process of perceiving and memorizing an actual scene is not that different from doing Old Master memory sketches, there are some differences.

Besides being static images, paintings are pre-composed. While you may be able to find an actual scene which is static, you will need to keep in mind the fact that it is not composed and framed. You may want to follow the practice of landscape painters who use framing-Ls, which are two, L-shaped pieces of matboard, to view the scene they are interested in. These allow you to frame the composition and to determine its proportions.

Another option is to decide, in advance, that you will restrict yourself to a specific aspect ratio or two. As an example, you could cut out a 2" x 3" rectangle from a piece of grey matboard. This device is called a *view-metre* and it restricts the framing of the scene to a pre-determined ratio.

It is best to choose natural scenes which are somewhat static so that you can return to them day after day. Even so, the lighting on the scene will likely be different between sessions. I recommend beginning these kinds of exercises just like the previous ones. On the first attempt, simply take in the visual impression, and on the second, analyze. Try not to get too discouraged as scene memorization is one of the most difficult processes.

To gather the impression, begin these exercises by simply staring at the image and letting the picture form in your mind. Fortunately, by now your ability to recall visual observations or impressions without analysis should be fairly well trained. Use your view-metre or a set of framing L's to bound the scene. Do your best to not think about the components which comprise the scene, simply let it wash over your field of view. After five minutes of this kind of simple observation, return to the studio and try to draw or paint the scene in greyscale.

Since these exercises are focused on value, I suggest using charcoal and white chalk on grey charcoal paper. Even though during this time you were not thinking about the value

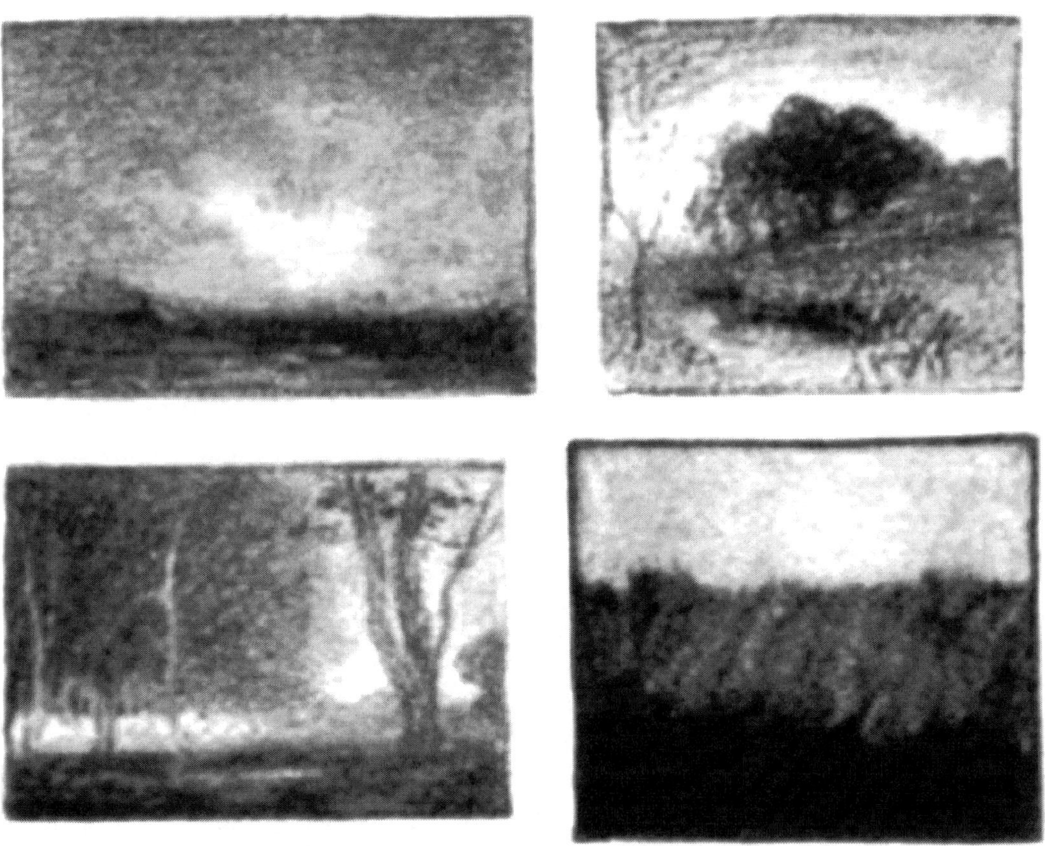

Landscape sketches from Poore's book on composition[4]

patterns in the scene, your mind perceived them. As charcoal is a mass-oriented medium, this aspect will help force you to approach the memory drawing with the "big look" in mind. Additionally, charcoal is less time consuming than paint, therefore it is more likely that these exercises will actually be attempted with some sort of regularity.

On the next day, bring your drawing with you when you return to the scene so that you can compare it to the source. After checking your work and noting the errors, set it aside and begin to analyze the actual scene, keeping your errors on the previous drawing in mind. During this analysis mode, one of the first things you should try to categorize are large patterns of value. Keep in mind that the sky is usually the lightest value, the ground-plane is usually a mid-tone and any vertical elements (like bushes and trees) are darker. These distinctions are often independent of the chiaroscuro aspects of light and shade. In fact, strong cast shadows often break the above rule. Analyze the scene for five to ten minutes, return to the studio and try another drawing. This time do your best to draw it via your analysis memory.

After shape memory exercises, scene memory is perhaps the most beneficial in the long term. If you can only commit to doing one memory-based task on a consistent basis, make it shape exercises. If you can consistently manage two, make this exercise the second one.

Advanced Value-Memory Exercises

The example image on the following pages is Jean-Léon Gérôme's painting, *The Dual After the Masquerade*. The source image, on the left-hand page, is simply a greyscale version of the painting. The image on the right-hand page is akin to what you are striving for with advanced value exercises.

These exercises are more difficult than scene-memory sketches due to the fact that you are after more than a general impression. With these you are trying for an exact, albeit simplified copy. You will spend four or five days memorizing the same image and working on the same drawing or painting. Another difference, as well as an additional difficulty, is that you will not check the result until the end of the last painting session. You may recall Degas' comment about his perfect atelier, from earlier in the book. Well, here is a chance to prove yourself in a way that he might deem appropriate.

- If in your regular art training you are painting, feel free to paint these exercises. If you are not painting yet, use charcoal.
- For value-memory exercises it is best to use greyscale images of paintings as your source rather than those reproduced in full color.
- Place the source on the wall or an easel four to six feet away.
- Stare at the source for ten minutes simply absorbing the image.
- When the timer goes off, put the source image out of sight and try to paint it from memory.
- You may draw the shapes from memory in pencil before painting or go straight in with paint. The latter is my preference.

- Work on the same memory drawing, once per day for four or five days.
- Do not compare your drawing or painting with your source until the end of the last day.

After copying the Gérôme, use any well-respected, Old Master painting you like. Try to choose simpler paintings at first, which have large areas of similar tones. It is helpful if

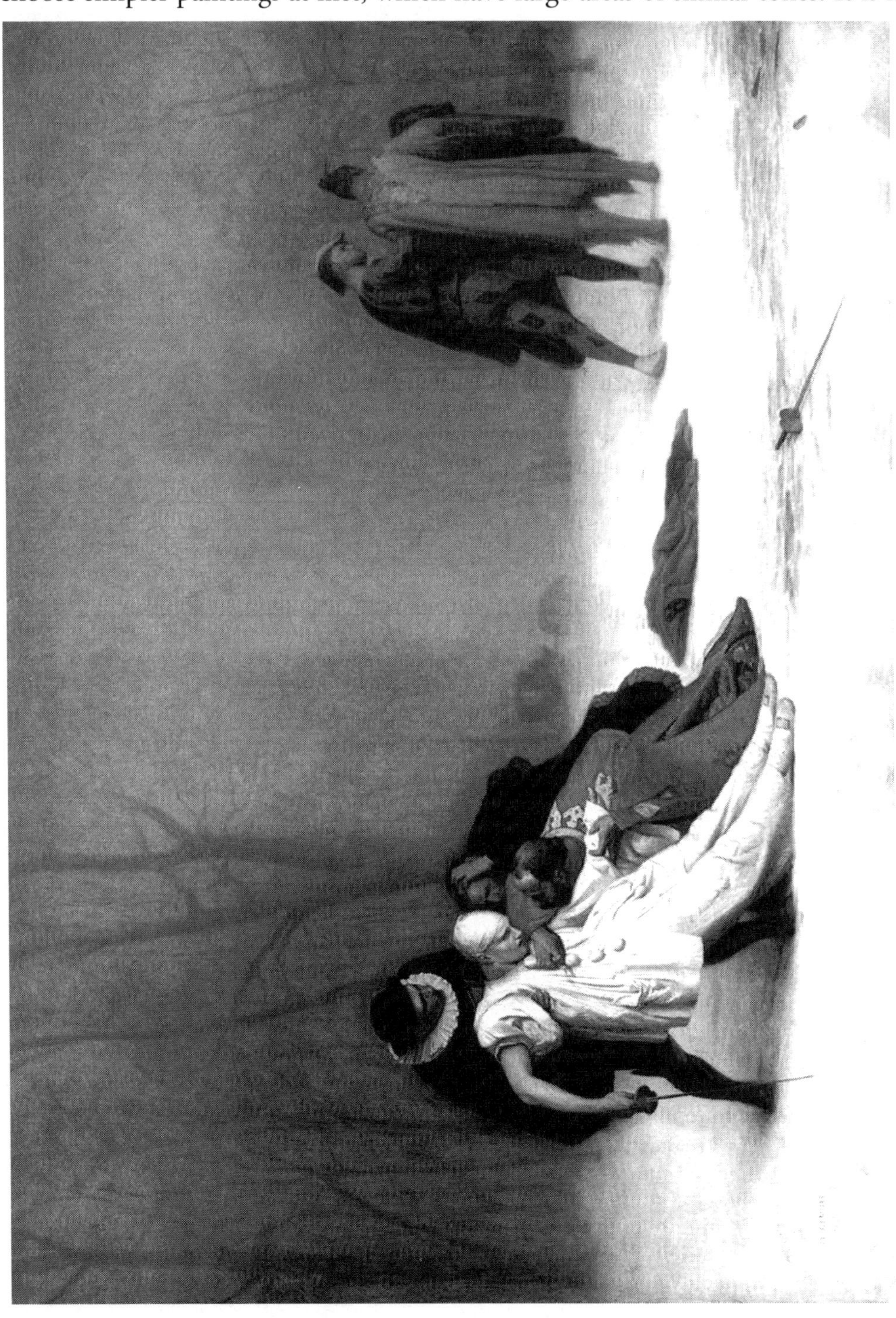

The Source Painting

the source is in greyscale. A good photocopy from a book or a black and white print from a computer ought to work well. After doing a few at four or five days per painting, and if you have proved your ability yo be accurate, drop to three days for the next painting. Then drop to two days and finally to one.

1 Poore, Henry, *Pictorial Composition and the Critical Judgment of Pictures*, (London: G. P. Putnam's Sons, 1903), 17.
2 *Ibid.*, Page 128.
3 *Ibid.*, Page 128.
4 *Ibid.*, Pages 119-120.

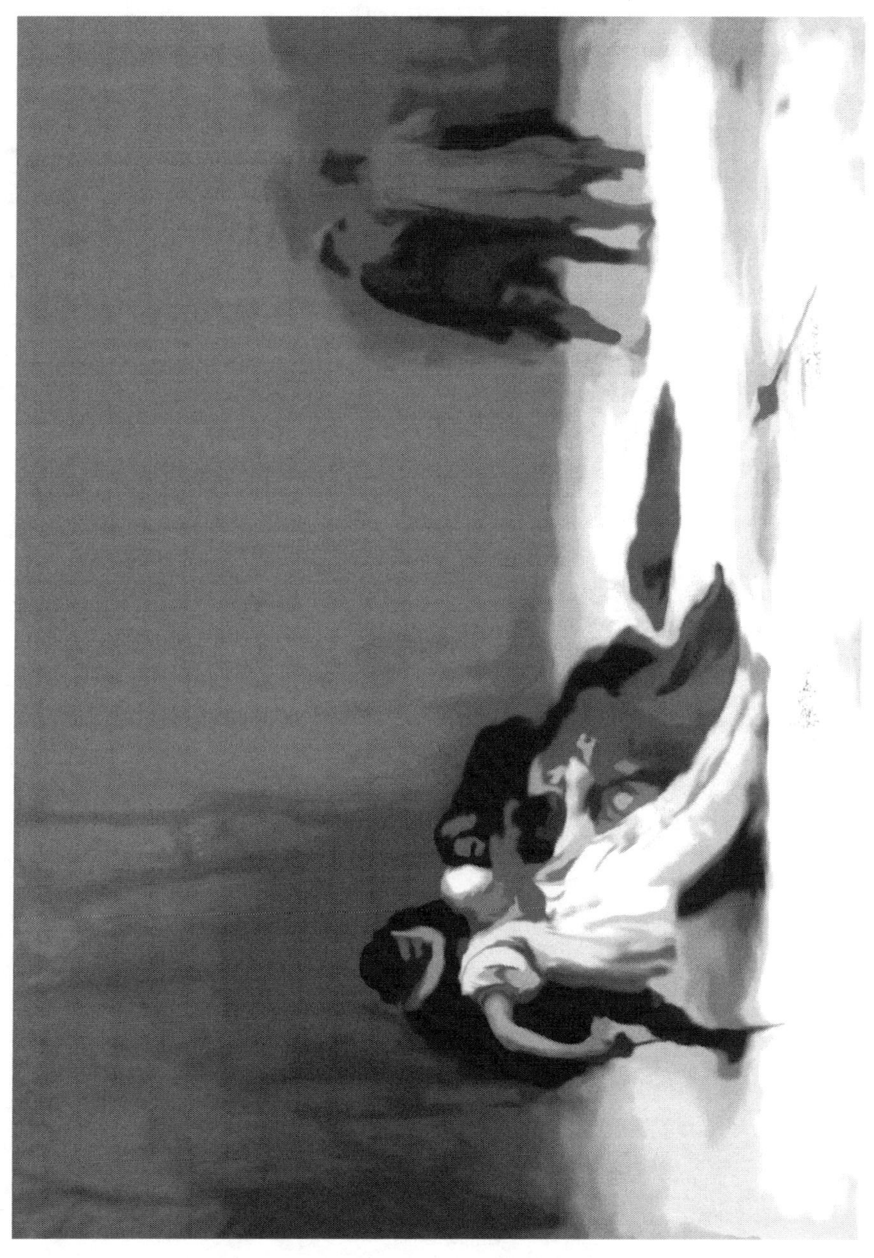

The Memory Result

Remember

- Every so often, reread the chapter on process.
- Focus your attention on the subject you are trying to memorize. Distractions and inattention are the biggest hindrances to memory.
- Close one eye.
- Remember that individual values are irrelevant. It is the relationship between the values that you are trying to perceive and recall.
- Rehearse the image. During the memorizing portion of the session, close your eyes now and then and try to form the image in your mind.
- For all exercises but the value squares, every so often physically trace image in the air with your finger and then close your eyes and trace it again.
- Pretend that you are painting the scene and think about how you would mix the values.
- When you are analyzing, begin with the large characteristics of the image and how they relate to each other.
- Now and then, verbally describe the value patterns out loud.
- Review your attempts every week and again every month, looking for errors which you consistently make. Learn from these mistakes by thinking about them during the future exercises. For example, if you tend to make the values too dark, spend more time observing the dark values in relation to the lights.
- Every so often wait an hour or more between the end of the viewing time and when you do the memory drawing. During this wait period, go about your daily activities and at the same time think about the image you tried to memorize. After the wait period is over, try to draw or paint the image as you normally would from your memory.
- Ongoing exercises may be found through a link on this website: http://www.memorydrawing.com.

·Color·

For even while I dwell in darkness and silence, in my memory I can produce colors, if I will, and discern betwixt black and white, and what others I will: nor yet do sounds break in and disturb the image drawn in by my eyes. . . -Saint Augustine[1]

If you are an atelier or self-study student who has yet to begin projects in color, I would suggest that you continue doing shape and value exercises. Let color memory work wait until you have some training and experience in observing and mixing color relationships.

Color presents our visual perception and memory with additional aspects to consider. Boisbaudran, Richard Lack, myself and others have noticed that students are not equally skilled between the ability to remember shape and value and the ability to remember color. Part of this is due to the fact that the perception of accurate color relationships is a more complex process than that for shape or value perception. Beyond the observational aspects is the additional problem of the gamut range of the medium being used.

Visual-perceptual learning is a process whereby one learns to visually perceive the differences between the parts of a given subject or between subjects.[2] In many ways, this is the analytical part of all of the previous exercises in this book. Having said that, the better one learns to perceive, the more likely it is that analysis will happen automatically and without conscious effort. Once again, regarding visual memory, one cannot recall was has not first been perceived.

All of this applies to learning to see and recall color. The teaching tradition I come from believes that only so much color perception may actually be able to be learned however, and the hard truth may be that the student either can or cannot perceive. Those who take this view believe that this is a physiological issue, and therefore training can only help to a certain extent.[3] This is not necessarily a tragedy however, because successful color in a painting is more often a matter of achieving accurate color *relationships* than strictly accurate color notes.

Although there are other philosophies, I maintain that the important thing to be aware of when perceiving color is that color is best perceived via the relationship of the color-note in question to the other notes which surround it.

If you recall the section on gestalt theory in the science chapter, this way of seeing color will seem familiar. In fact, there is some solid science behind the theory as the cones in our eyes work in just this way.[4]

Even though gestaltism was never mentioned to me by any of my teachers, the principle of *simultaneous contrast* and the idea of perceiving a color in relation to the colors which surround it are related. According to R. H. Ives Gammell,

> *When we focus our eyes on a single detail which lies in our field of vision, we see an actual, or local, color whose hue can be readily matched with paint. Now most painters have been content to paint their pictures in tones deliberately or subconsciously derived from these local colors blended into a brownish sauce. Variants of this custom have prevailed ever since oil painting came into general use during the fifteenth century. But the impressionists, with Titian as their precursor, gradually discovered that the mysterious beauty of the visible world which ravished them resided in the interrelationship of its constituent colors. In order to convey this overall impression, the painter must put down the colors as they appear to his trained eye when he views the area to be depicted in its entirety, as a unit. The resulting colors will differ markedly from the tones observed singly.*[5]

When I was in school I was taught to see color relationships, not color. When critiquing my work, my teacher would stand back and observe my subject right alongside my painting. When he noticed an error, he would take my palette and mix the correct color note. Often, he would even go so far as to repaint the area in question. During the process he would look at the subject in a number of different ways, and, of those, the two most helpful to me were *looking away* and *blurring*. I would then look at his corrections and compare them to nature. Through these comparisons, between my observations and his corrections, over time I began to perceive the correct color notes and their relationships accurately to nature.*

Looking Away

One of the keys to observing color relationships is to not look directly at the color in question. It is better to focus an inch or two above the entire scene and try to see the whole of it peripherally instead. Then, focus a similar distance above your painting to see whether your painting holds together in the same way that nature does.

Although it is more applicable to observing shape errors, you may also find it helpful to quickly flick your eye between the two areas (above the scene and above the painting). However, when looking away, areas of the scene can be so far away from the central cone of your vision that your ability to perceive them is somewhat compromised.

Another approach is to focus slightly away from the specific area in question, first within the scene and then on your painting.

*Although not exclusive to sight-size, the process described above is more fully fleshed out in my previous books, *Cast Drawing Using the Sight-Size Approach* and *Cast Painting Using the Sight-Size Approach.*

Blurring

The other color perception technique I was taught to use was to blur my eyes. Just as when looking away, blurring helps you to see the scene as a whole, rather than in a piecemeal fashion. The difference between blurring and looking away is that when blurring you are looking, more or less, at the center of the scene. If you are near-sighted, you may have an advantage because you can remove your glasses. Of course, if your eyes are bad enough, without your glasses you may see things too blurred to be of much help.

Blurring your eyes is not something everyone can do at will but there is another way to achieve the same effect. I am certain that most are aware of the caricature of an artist closing one eye, holding his thumb up and staring at it. As comical as that image is, there is some truth to it. When you focus on your raised thumb, everything else within your field of view is progressively blurred based upon how far away it is from your thumb.

These methods help your eye to perceive a broader field of vision and therefore the entirety of the color relationships within the scene. Feel free to look directly at the source sometimes as well, just be sure to spend some time simply taking in the peripheral, unfocused visual impression.

Warm and Cool

An important concept to be aware of is how warm or cool a color is, relative to the surrounding colors. In this sense, evaluating a color is like evaluating a value, when we ask ourselves how light or dark something is compared to the other elements in the scene. When it comes to color, the questions are:

- Is the target color warmer or cooler than the surrounding colors?
- Is your attempt at mixing the color warmer or cooler than your target?

In the beginning this way of mixing color is clearly trial and error. However, this is an important part of learning how to perceive color *relationally*.

Although the concept of relative warmth and coolness is a central tenet of visual color impressions, the reader should be aware that these terms are now looked down upon in some circles due to their non-specific nature. Of course the same can be said regarding the terms "light" and "dark" as well as "soft" and "sharp." This is true enough. However, the point is that they are meant to describe relationships. Nonetheless, whether you find yourself in a class which teaches color perception via warm/cool or not, I cannot say this enough times, memorize color via color relationships rather than through isolated colors.

Color Gamut

Color-memory training begins with colored squares, just like value memory training, and the similarity does not end there. That does not mean that they are identical processes however. Practically speaking there are only so many perceptible value differences and even many greyscales are restricted to nine or ten discrete shades. The options for color are exponentially greater and simply wandering through the house paint section of the local hardware store will reveal that.

"Values first and the color will take care of itself" is something that I heard over and over again when I was in school. There are a number of reasons behind this adage but regarding memory drawing the main one is gamut. Although it is a complicated issue, the value gamut of your paint appears to more closely approximate nature than the color gamut does. In other words, in the exercises which follow it is better to err on the side of the proper value relationships of the colors.

Your medium of choice partly determines which color combinations you will be able to use for your exercises. The gamut of your paint must be able to approximate the source colors of the exercises, and due to this I suggest that you actually paint your sources yourself, in watercolor or oil, rather than rely on printed or digital sources. In this way you will confirm that your paint choices will be able to reach the color note you see in the source. A better solution would be to have someone else create the sources for you, with the kinds of paints you will be using.*

Another option is to use differently colored squares of construction paper, as long as you feel certain that your paint can match them. Or, head back to that hardware store and gather some of those house paint color sample strips. Just make sure that those sources are not beyond the gamut of your medium.

Creating Your Sources

To create the colored source squares, it is best to use a palette with few colors. The parameters of that limit are up to you. This could mean using a traditional, limited palette comprised mostly of earth tones or even a more Impressionistic one with both high- and low-chroma reds, yellows and blues. What matters is that you use the same set of colors when you are painting from memory.

Using your medium of choice (watercolor, oil, etc.), paint a series of differently mixed colors on 1" x 1" squares. Both oil and watercolor will work fine on watercolor paper, but oil may work better on primed matboard, canvas, canvas board or prepared paper. Shellacked, heavyweight paper also works well. You can vary any, or all of the properties of the colors (hue, value, chroma); just make sure that the resulting colored squares are flatly painted with no obvious value or color-shifts and that they are not too high in chroma.

Trying to reproduce color relationships from memory and from a matte source, is an additional complication. If you are using oil paint for the squares, add in some of your preferred painting medium (not simply a solvent) so that the paint dries without sinking-in. If it does sink-in after it dries, brush some oil or retouch varnish over it before you begin to use the squares for your memory work. I prefer that my students use oil, but if you use watercolor you will not have this problem.

I suggest making twenty to thirty differently colored squares, each in low to medium-chroma (not starkly saturated). Having this many sources will allow you to vary the number of squares to be memorized in a session and to be able to vary the combinations. Once they are dry, cut them out with a scissors. Wait a week before you begin to do the exercises so

*If you are learning color ordering via Munsell squares, feel free to use those, just remember to use more than one square at a time for each exercise. Once again, you are training your ability to perceive and recall color *relationships*, rather than independent color notes.

that whatever memory you had of their creation can fade. Be sure to number the backs of each square, but their numerical order does not matter.

Creating the Background

The background surrounding the colored squares is as important as the colored squares themselves. The easiest thing to use is white paper. Easy is not always best however, and using white as a background can result in too dramatic a contrast between the squares and the background. Furthermore, the bright white may actually impede your ability to memorize the colors of the squares due to a possible afterimage.

It is far better to use a mid-tone grey as a background value. Of course the grey background on your memory painting should be the same as what is behind your memory source. To assure this you should create *blanks* upon which you will paint your exercises.

Using a ruler, draw ten pairs of 1" x 1" squares directly next to each other onto the same kind of support that you used for the previously painted source squares. These squares will be your blanks. Next, create ten more sets, only this time draw three 1" x 1" squares for each set. Finally, create another set of ten, but with four squares instead of three. Cut all of the sets out, but not the individual squares, and set them aside.

When it comes time to do the exercises, you will tape the backs of your source squares to a mid-toned sheet of grey paper. You will then tape the back of your blank sets to a similar grey sheet. The sheet serves as background for both your source and your painting.

Process

Just as with the value-memory exercises, you will alternate using a constant square. This means that the first time you work on an exercise you should paint one of the squares while actually looking at it.* This painted square is the constant. Then, for the second time through on the following day, try it without using the pre-painted reference square. This time memorize its color as well. Alternate in this way for each week's exercise.

In the beginning, choose squares which are differently contrasted, not simply in value but also in their hue. Then, as you are more successful in memorizing their relationships, choose squares which are progressively closer in their appearance. This process helps to train your perception, and therefore your memory, for subtle variations in color.

Again when you are memorizing the squares try to memorize them as a whole unit by perceiving the color notes of the squares as they relate to each other, not simply as independent agents.

- Tape the back of a pair of exercise square blanks to a sheet of neutral grey paper and set it aside. This is what you will paint the exercise on.
- Tape the backs of a paired set of previously painted source squares to a sheet of the same kind of neutral grey paper.
- Tack the sheet to the wall or an easel and stand back a few feet.
- The first time through choose one of the squares to serve as your constant.

*Instead of actually painting the constant, when the time comes to paint from your memory, you could simply use the square itself by actually placing it next to the square you are trying to paint.

- Set the timer for five minutes. As your memory for color improves, try three minutes regardless of how many squares you are memorizing.
- Stare at the source image, comparing its color to the reference square.
- At times, stare slightly above the squares and/or blur your eyes, trying to take in the visual impression of the whole.
- When the timer goes off, put the source image out of sight.
- Try to paint the target square from memory onto your prepared blank support.
- Be sure to use the constant square as a relative guide.
- To check your memory drawing for accuracy, place it directly next to, above or below the source image and stand back. Then, flick your eye back and forth between the source and your painting. You may want to squint down and flick your eye again. You should see no difference between the source and your exercise.
- Number and date the back of your exercise squares with their matching source numbers. This will allow you to compare them to their source when you review at a later date.
- On every other day, alternate your use of the constant reference square with memorizing it.
- Use each set until your color accuracy improves, but no longer than a week, then go onto the next set.
- Once you achieve consistent success with pairs, go onto triplets, etc.
- Every so often wait an hour or more between the end of the viewing time and when you do the memory drawing. During this wait period, go about your daily activities and at the same time think about the image you tried to memorize. After the wait period is over, try to paint the image as you normally would from your memory.

Learn From Your Mistakes

Improvement in your color perception and memory is not merely a matter of practice. Yes, practice is important, but at some point you will be repeating what you have learned and at that point your learning curve may very well plateau. This is inevitable, and it not only happens with color memory, it happens with shape and value memory as well.

The best remedy is to figure out if and where you consistently make errors and to then focus on those issues. After you finish all of the color square exercises, go through them with a critical eye and set aside all that are less than perfect, including their sources (this is where the numbered backs will help). What do you notice? Is there a color-range that you can't seem to match all of the time- or ever? Is the error because of the color itself? As an example, do you have more difficulty with colors in the red end of the spectrum? Are most of the errors happening with sources with less contrast? Errors like these may be corrected by focusing on a number of exercises which are similar to the ones in which you had the problems.

If you notice a lot of errors, it may be indicative of problems in your perception rather than in your memory. As we have seen, perception needs to precede memory for that memory to be accurate. These kinds of errors may indicate that you may have some form of color deficiency or you may simply have a difficult time visually separating distinct colors. Unfortunately, deficiencies cannot likely be corrected if they are the result of a genetic or physical condition.[6]

Just because you created the sources yourself, does not mean that you can discern the difference between every given set. One way to determine whether your color perception ability is lacking is to try and paint the sets on which you erred, directly from their sources rather than from your memory. If you are unable to succeed with that, you cannot expect to succeed when memorizing them. The issue may then be in your ability to accurately mix the colors you perceive. This problem could simply be inexperience, and you may want to keep to a more limited number of colors until you become more proficient at color mixing.

Advanced Color Memory

The later exercises in the chapter on value memory involved memorizing Old Master compositions. The same kind of thing should be done in color. Follow the process that I previously described in the section about Old Master Memory Sketches (on page 84), only this time do them in color. The following is a snippet from that chapter, reworded so it relates to color:

> *These Old Master memory sketches should represent the main shapes in the source painting in terms of simple color-value patterns. . . Sketching scenes from memory is doing just that, delineating the large patterns of discrete color-value.*

I will make some more suggestions regarding advanced color memory in the next chapter. For now, however, students should spend much more time on memorizing form (shape and value) than on memorizing color.[7]

---

1 Saint Augustine, Bishop of Hippo. *The Confessions of Saint Augustine, Book X.* Translated by Edward Bouverie Pusey.
2 Özgen, Emre and Davies, Ian R. L. "Acquisition of Categorical Color Perception: A Perceptual Learning Approach to the Linguistic Relativity Hypothesis," *Journal of Experimental Psychology,* Vol. 131, no. No. 4 (2003): 478.
3 To test your ability to perceive color (hue) differences, take this online test: http://www.xrite.com/custom_page. aspx?PageID=77
4 "Consider an intense beam of blue light, surrounded by white light, striking our retinas. Where the blue light strikes, the blue cones will be stimulated, overloaded and fatigued. The horizontal cells that link the blue cones will cause blue cones, outside of but close to the blue beam, to also become fatigued. In the surround of the blue beam where the white light falls, the blue receptors will be fatigued and the white light will appear to our brain as yellow. (Recall that blue light plus yellow light equals white light.) Simultaneous contrast causes the white around the blue to seem yellow. Similarly, white light around a yellow beam will seem blue." See http://www.webexhibits.org/colorart/contrast.html (retrieved on 12 Dec 2012).
5 Gammell, R. H. Ives. "Chardin Today," *Classical Realism Quarterly,* October 28, 1991, Vol. VI, No. 1, page 5.
6 See http://en.wikipedia.org/wiki/Color_blindness.
7 Lack, Richard F. "Memory Training For Painters." *Classical Realism Quarterly.* V.2 (1990): 20.

Remember

- Every so often reread the chapter on process.
- Focus your attention on the subject you are trying to memorize. Distractions and inattention are the biggest hindrances to memory.
- Close one eye.
- Alternate staring directly at the image with looking at it somewhat peripherally.
- If you are able, now and then blur your eyes when looking at the source.
- Remember that individual color notes are irrelevant. It is the relationship between the notes that you are trying to perceive and recall.
- Rehearse the image, meaning, during the memorizing portion of the session, close your eyes now and then and try to form the image in your mind.
- Try to imagine how you would mix the colors being observed.
- "Paint" the image in the air with your finger, both while observing it and then with your eyes closed.
- Now and then, verbally describe the color patterns out loud.
- Review your attempts every week and again every month, looking for errors which you consistently make. Learn from these mistakes by thinking about them during the future exercises. As an example, if you tend to make the colors too warm, spend more time observing the temperature relationships between the colors.
- Every so often wait an hour or more between the end of the viewing time and when you do the memory drawing. During this wait period, go about your daily activities and at the same time think about the image you tried to memorize. After the wait period is over, try to paint the image as you normally would from your memory.
- Ongoing exercises may be found through a link on this website: http://www.memorydrawing.com.

·Advanced Memory Drawing·

You need to draw using your eye, that is, imprint everything in your mind . . .[1]
-Gian Lorenzo Bernini

The following is what Richard Lack believed the advanced student should be doing at this stage in their training:

> *The next stage of memory work involves the study of nature - the world of three-dimensional space. I do not recommend starting this until a student can memorize complicated subjects from the flat, and match colors with a great deal of accuracy. At this stage a student must show proficiency in drawing from nature, i.e. seeing proportions correctly, understanding how light and shadow give forms relief, and having at least a rudimentary ability to state true color from indoor subjects such as a still life. Here memory work is only limited by the student's imagination. . . The student can then start to memorize objects from the everyday world such as a chair in the corner, a cat sitting in a window, a face seen on a bus, even a "talking head" from a television program. These drawings can be done in a small sketchbook kept solely for that purpose. The medium could be pen, pencil, felt marker, or whatever the student feels comfortable using. Quite naturally, these sketches will not be highly finished, but they will demonstrate the value of working from memory.*[2]

As Lack mentions, advanced memory work, especially in color, should only be undertaken by students who have demonstrated their abilities when working directly from nature.

Cast, Still Life, Figure and Portraiture from Memory

Cast, still life, figure and portrait painting represent the main division of subjects in most modern-day ateliers. They are naturally done from life and I do not mean to alter that process. However, advanced students have much to gain by painting these subjects from memory. As long as their studies from life continue, I suggest trying to do complete memory paintings of these subjects every so often. After the student masters cast painting from life, they should spend a week or two trying to paint a simple cast from memory. The same goes for still life, figure and portraiture. These memory paintings should not merely be sketches, but inasmuch as possible, the student should strive to make them finished paintings. Fully-trained artists might try this now and then as well.

The best way to approach something like this is to set up the subject in a different room than where you will be painting it. This arrangement requires that you travel between the rooms to get a look at the subject. Do you remember Degas' dream academy?

> *If I were to open an academy I would have a five-story building. The model would pose on the ground floor with the first-year students. The most advanced students would work on the fifth floor.*[3]

However, let me be clear once again. As valuable as this kind of study is, it should not replace your painting from life. Degas might not agree, but then again his own training was not as he later recommended to others.

Memory from Landscape

Landscape painters may arguably have the most to gain from a trained visual memory. Birge Harrison, in his book *Landscape Painting*, comments as follows:

> *There is no man, probably, who has more need of the help of this faithful sub-conscious servant than the artist, for so many of the mental processes of art must be instinctive. Moreover, in the purely mechanical sense, painters, and especially landscape painters, are peculiarly dependent upon a well trained memory.*[4]

He even went so far as to claim that a landscape, *"Must always be painted from memory."*[5] This statement seems to mirror George Inness' belief as well. However, Harrison later tempers it, but just slightly:

> *Of course one must paint what one sees, but one must see through the mind as well as through the eye. I do not mean by this to assert that young painters can entirely dispense with study direct from nature, or even that the veteran would not do well occasionally to carry his easel into the open air. The student indeed must paint for many years direct from his subject, must pry as closely as ever he can into the secrets of nature; but I would have him at the same time constantly train the sub-conscious servant, so that when the time comes that his services shall be needed, he will be indeed a 'good and faithful servant.'*[6]

I personally enjoy painting directly from nature so much that I consider memory to be an assistant, not the other way around. However, whether you agree that landscape, or any subject, must "always" be done from memory, try to train yourself like it must.

Landscape Memory Color Sketching

If you have followed this book's lessons in sequence, you should already have some experience doing value-memory sketches from landscape scenes. I will also assume that you have some landscape painting experience - direct from life. If you do not, you may be better off continuing with value-memory landscape sketching until you do.

It is now time to introduce color into these exercises, and as I suggested in the value chapter, you would do best to choose scenes which can be returned to again and again. To help assure this, take a look at the weekly weather forecast before venturing out. If possible, choose two or three days in a row, or within the same week, that have similar forecasts.

As with other memory drawing subjects, you should approach landscape-memory sketching in two sequential ways: impression, then analysis. Impression should always come first because once you begin to analyze a scene it is very hard to go back to impression. Analysis tends to take over.

Once again, use your framing-Ls or view-metre in order to help you to compose the scene. Now and then squint down and look for the abstract patterns which are present. Try not to think, "That's a tree, a rock, a river." Spend about ten minutes and then head back to the studio and try to paint the scene in whatever colored medium with which you are most comfortable. Do not expect to create a masterpiece but remember that it is merely an exercise. It is OK for these early sketches to be very simplified and nondescript.

The next day that lighting conditions are similar will be your analysis day. Be sure to take your previous day's sketch with you and compare it to nature, noting the discrepancies and then put it out of sight. Keep these errors in mind while you are memorizing the scene during this session.

The first step in analysis is to simplify the scene into three sections: horizontal (ground plane), vertical (trees, etc.) and sky. Just like the day before, squint down and think about what shapes those are and how they relate to each other. How would they fit together as puzzle pieces? Once again, look for the abstract patterns which are present in the scene. Since you had already memorized this scene, these patterns should seem familiar. Try to determine the relative values and colors for each of the three sections and all of the abstract shapes.

Now is the proper time to think, "Cloud, tree, lake, etc." Feel free to actually name what you see out loud. Close your eyes and do this as well, then open them and search the scene for what you named. If any part of the scene looks remotely like something else, note it in your mind, e.g., the arabesque of the biggest tree looks like a chicken.

While you are analyzing, try to paint the scene in your head. What colors would you mix? How would you go about laying in the painting? What would you paint next?

After ten minutes, turn away and go back to the studio and paint the memory. On the way back, try to visualize the scene and speak its characteristics out loud.

Color Gamut in Landscape Painting

Landscape painting again brings up the question of gamut. In controlled studio conditions the gamut differences between nature and oil paint are not usually off by that much. Outside, however, is a much different story altogether. Gamut is one of the reasons beginners struggle with landscape painting, from life as well as from their memory.

Beginning with the darks is oftentimes the best choice as oil paint can more closely approximate that end of the color-value range than the lights. As an example, it is true that pure, white paint is very bright. However, few things in nature are white and many things are brighter than even the lightest white paint. Trying to maintain that bright value while adding any amount of color to it is impossible.

Whether for the purposes of memory or from life, establish the extremes first. After determining the darkest areas it is best to try to observe the larger masses of color-value. Others prefer to begin with horizon, noting how the sky and land vary along its path. Either of these options should help keep you in gamut.

The All-Pervading Hue

Another consideration is the general color of the light on the scene. Who hasn't noticed the quality of the light just before sunset? Landscape painters call this time the "golden hour." It is called *golden,* not only because of its brilliance, but because of its hue which is generally an orange-yellow. It is most noticeable near the edges of the day, at sunrise and sunset.

During other times of day, the all-pervading hue is less noticeable, unless you look for it, because the intensity of the sky is often overpowering. If you are observant however and know what to look for you will notice a distinct blue-tint to upward facing surfaces. Reflections off clouds and other atmospheric conditions can envelope the landscape in other hues as well. Part of a landscape painter's job, whether for the purposes of memory or not, is to capture the all-pervading hue that is present in the scene before them.

Scenes with People

Now is the time to begin alternating the memory drawing exercises from your studio figure-drawing sessions with live-scene images that contain people. This will be more difficult because unlike the figure-drawing exercises, you will not have the memory of drawing the real world scenes first. Spend some time staring at an actual scene at the shopping mall or a restaurant. When you return home try to draw that scene from your memory. Eventually, begin to do these in paint and in full color.

At this stage, static scenes, like people sitting in a cafe, will be more easily studied and recalled than moving ones. Obviously, there is no convenient way to check your accuracy although one could take a photograph of the scene during the observation time. Be careful though, the ease of this kind of photography, not to mention its artlessness, may hinder your progress. Knowing you have a photo available can also result in it becoming a crutch.

Final Suggestions

Memory drawing does not have to remain a formal endeavour. Maintenance, as well as improvement, can and should happen informally. Quick, thumbnail memory sketching can be done almost anywhere and from any recent observation. As Richard Lack wrote, *"Memory work is only limited by the student's imagination."*[7]

1 Cited in *Bernini: Sculpting in Clay*, New York: The Metropolitan Museum of Art, 2012), 65.

2 Lack, Richard F. "Memory Training For Painters." *Classical Realism Quarterly*. V.2 (1990): 20.

3 *Degas* by Henri Hertz, Felix Alcan, Paris, 1920, as quoted in Gammell, R. H. Ives. *The Shop-talk of Edgar Degas*. Boston: University Press, 1961.

4 Harrison, Birge. *Landscape Painting*. New York: Charles Scribner's Sons, 1909. Page 168.

5 *Ibid.*, Page 171.

6 *Ibid.*, Page 172.

7 Lack, *op. cit.*, Page 20.

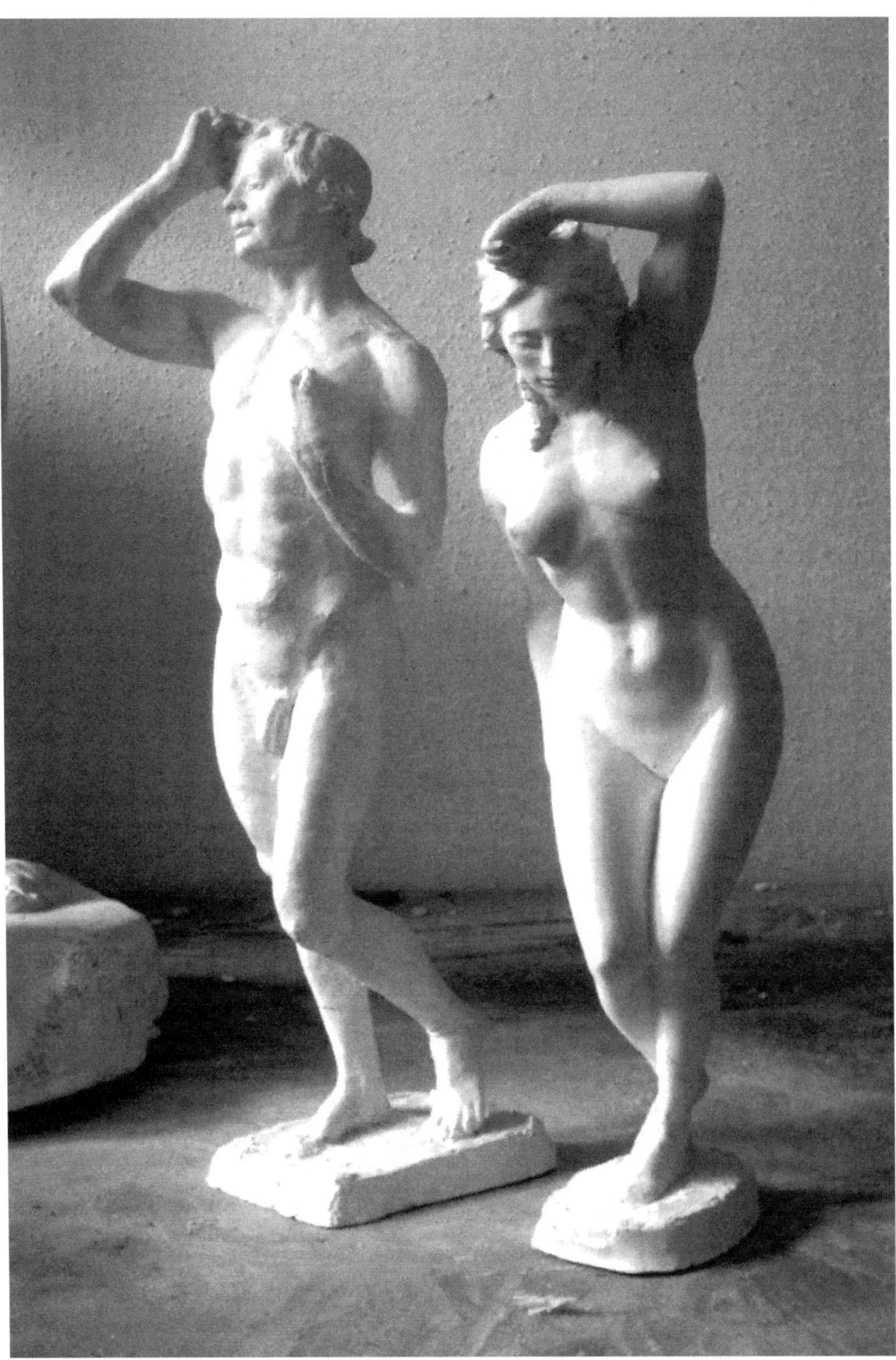

Expulsion -by Matthew J. Collins. This plaster is a work done largely from memory. To see more of Matthew's sculptures as well as his drawings, paintings and etchings, be sure to check out his website: http://matthewjamescollins.com.

·Sculptural Memory·

I learned to draw a great deal from memory and thus I learned to observe; this has always proved useful to me . . .[1]   -Auguste Rodin

Sculptors who create figurative pieces draw as much as any other artist. They also use their visual memory in similar ways. In fact, they may even need a more fully developed visual memory because their creations exist in three-dimensions as opposed to two. With the possible exception of the chapter on color, sculptors would be wise to do most of the preceding exercises in this book, including those in the chapter on value. In this chapter Matthew Collins and I offer some suggestions for additional exercises. Readers who are not sculpture students may also benefit from doing these exercises.

Art Comes From Art

It can be difficult to explain the process that a trained artist goes through when working from memory. Too many think that the only point of training one's memory is to be able to close your eyes and copy a picture in your mind. It is true that this is one of the goals for memory-drawing exercises, but it not the ultimate goal of memory training.

Matthew's process in developing his figurative, sculptural work is heavily dependent upon his visual memory. Each piece is usually born out of a single idea, an observed gesture or pose. After doing a few thumbnail sketches from life, he begins modeling in clay. He then combines his knowledge of construction, anatomy and other art he has seen, with a mental image in his memory in order to complete the sculpture.

An artist's accumulated visual memory includes his or her intimate familiarity with the art of the past. Those forms, along with nature, inform the work that they create. Art often comes from art. Passages of Matthew's sculptures are at times inspired by his memories of other sculptures. For example, he might work up a foot based on what he previously saw in a sculpture by Bartolini. Models are then brought in to enrich certain parts which require more information to complete.

Matthew believes that his visual memory, imagination and his personal artistic voice combine to create a single expressive force. This belief is exemplified in his works.

E Pluribus Unum - Out of Many, One

Shape is contour and relative to sculpture, the shape is comprised of many contours. When a sculptor rotates the sculpture-stand, he is often looking at the overall contour of the sculpture. The completed piece is a compilation of a multitude of these views. If you can get all of these contours correct, from enough angles of view, you have a fully realized sculpture. Here again we see the "big look" in action.

The multitude of views does present a problem. It is not possible to see from more than one viewpoint at a time, and therefore sculptors need to visualize what they do not immediately see in their subject. This visualization can happen in either of the two ways that I described in the chapter on science: top-down or bottom-up. During the process of sculpting, the sculptor thinks about the construction of the shape, its visual appearance, and very often both.

Separating Observed Fact From Conceptual Fiction*

Throughout this book I have consistently pointed out that to fully train your visual memory you need to follow two approaches: perception and analysis. Cleanly separating these is difficult enough for the painter. For the sculptor it may be more difficult because visualizing anatomy and construction is simply a natural part of the sculptural process.

What is not immediately affected by concept is one's initial glimpse of a fleeting subject. This is as true for two-dimensions as for three. If you have been diligent, the previous exercises should have built up your perceptual-memory abilities to the extent that you are now quite skilled in recalling the visual aspects of things which you only briefly see.

Mental Rotation

Although not designed specifically for the purpose, a test of one's abilities to comprehend the shape of an image without relying on concept is the Shepard & Metzler mental rotation task.[2] The test works as follows. The subject is presented with a series of images. All of the images are of the same object or shape, except for one, and each image is rotated differently from the first. The goal of the test is to discern which rotated object is not the same.

Take a look at the images on the following page. Which object is not the same as the others? The answer is at the end of this chapter.

One of the ways to strengthen your ability to recall three-dimensional shapes without relying on recognition is to use nondescript objects as your source material. These could be anything from small, irregularly-shaped rocks, to larger boulders, to tree stumps. It is not important what the source is, in fact, the less recognizable the better.

In the beginning, choose an object that is around the size of a baseball. Make sure that it is an irregular shape. Set it on a white paper plate, under good light. Stare at it for five minutes, rotating the plate now and then. Do not touch the object. You are trying to strengthen your visual perception and memory, not your tactile memory. When the time is finished, remove the object from view. Take some modeling clay and try to mould it into the shape of the object you recall.

*Concept, like all constructive and anatomical approaches, has its original basis in observed fact. However, nature consistently deviates from those general facts when it comes to the specific. Proof of this is exemplified in *likeness*. For you to appear different from me, the specifics of the forms of your face have to be different from mine.

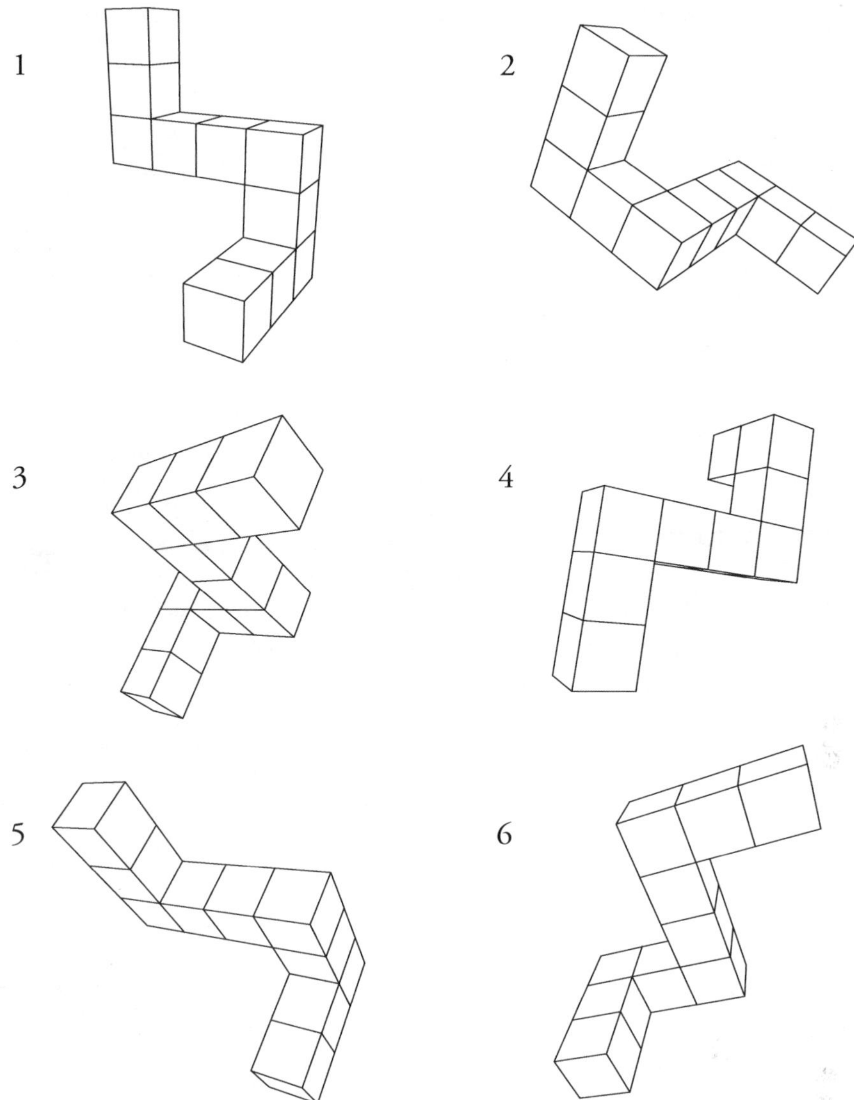

Checking for errors will not be as simple as it is with two-dimensional work. In addition to visually comparing the objects, try holding the source in one of your hands and your sculpture in the other. Make certain that they are oriented the same in each hand. Gently rotate the object and your sculpture around to get a sense of their physical likeness. If this is too difficult to manage, you could try holding one at a time, alternating between each one.

I suggest doing these abstract mental-rotation exercises every so often.

Memory Maquettes

Many sculptors create clay maquettes, which are small thumbnail models of what the final sculpture will look like. They are akin to the painter's thumbnail sketches. Making maquettes from memories of things that you have previously observed is a staple of sculptural-memory training.

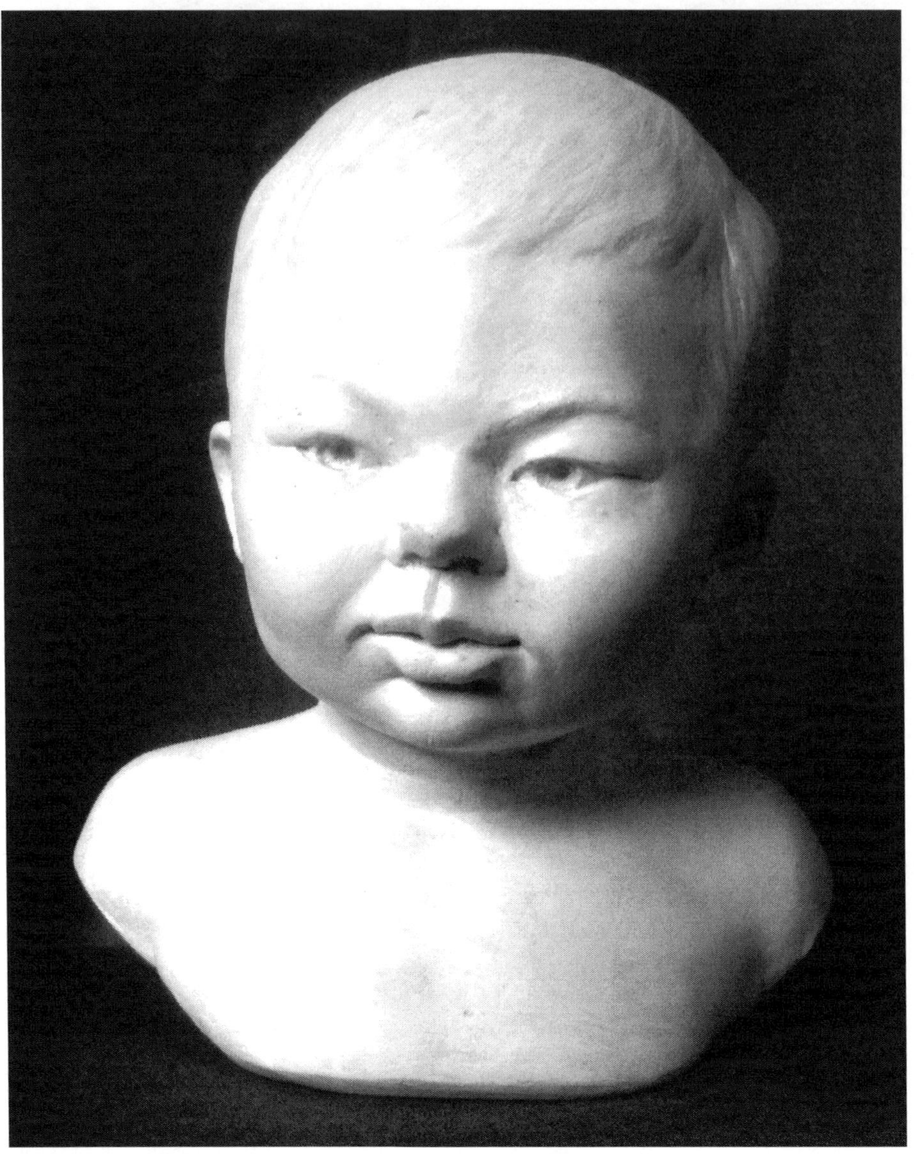

Gabriel at 9 Months -by Matthew J. Collins. Plaster. This bust of Matthew's nine-month-old son was done from a mixture of life-study and memory.

The best sources for these memory maquettes are things which are static. If you have access to a skeleton, work your way through the major bones. Children's toys may be fine sources, but they are often not the most aesthetically pleasing. The more uncommon the object is, the better, as you will be less inclined to use your knowledge of the object to cheat your memory. When you become more proficient, the human figure will be more useful, although animals may work as well.

Whatever the source, make sure that you can view it from multiple angles and that you can see it again once your memory maquette is done. Spend no more than ten minutes observing the subject. Make sure to view it all the way around.

When the time is up, go into another room and try to sculpt the object from your memory. After you have made your best effort, go back to the source and compare. If the subject is complicated, use the same source for a week. There is some benefit to working on the same maquette over the course of the week but make that the exception. For the most part, do a new maquette, even when you are using the same object as your source.

If you do figure drawing in school, and you have been drawing these from memory in the evenings, try to occasionally do one in modeling clay instead. This could be done once, or many times on the same maquette.

Sculptors would do well to continue exercising their memory via drawing. Given their training, they will see things in a way that two-dimensional artists normally do not.

(The answer to the mental rotation test is #4.)

1 As quoted in Albert Edward Elsen, *Auguste Rodin: Readings on His Life and Work,* (New York: Prentice-Hall, 1965), 169-170.
2 The mental-rotation test is based upon Shepard & Metzler's Rotation Task. See Shepard, Roger N., and Jacqueline Metzler, 'Mental Rotation of Three-Dimensional Objects,' 1971 *Science*, 171. no. 3972: pp. 701-703.

Appendix I

•Sage Advice from Père Lecoq•

This appendix is a reprint of the main part of Appendix I of Boisbaudran's book, *The Training of the Memory in Art and the Education of the Artist.*

In observing a subject there are five principal points to be kept in view. They are: dimensions, position, form, modeling, and color.

To observe the dimensions or proportions, compare the different parts of the subject one with another, and choose one as a unit of measure.

To appreciate the respective position of the different parts, imagine horizontal and vertical lines passing through the most noticeable points. These lines and their points of intersection once established, will give the memory exact landmarks from which to make definite observation.

In calculating a shape, one may imagine it inscribed in a simple elementary figure, such as a square, a circle, a triangle, etc., and decide how far it approaches or recedes from the imaginary figure described about it. These principles are those of ordinary drawing, it is only a matter of applying them to memory work.

Modeling, which comprises the advancement and retirement of form, is best observed by comparing with each other the different tones that result from the varying quantity of light and shade. Some part of the subject, either the darkest or the lightest, should be used as a unit of comparison.

For color observation, it is necessary to judge and compare with each other both the different values of light and shade, and the different degrees of intensity of color. And here the memory can fill the very important office of recalling with absolute fidelity the tints chosen as units of comparison. They are the fixed points from which to calculate the intensity of the other colors.

It is especially in the early stages of memory work that my pupils make use of these general methods, together with personal methods of their own invention. But as practice develops the power of seeing the object though no longer present, such conscious methods become gradually less necessary. For then the proportions, points, shapes, modeling, and color are calculated by what I may call the inner eye of the memory, without recourse to previous calculations and reasoning, much as they are judged by the eye in ordinary vision.

To see the object, when absent, is then the real goal to which all these exercises should lead. Among the various methods of procedure which may help directly to this result, I will mention only one of the most successful. Here, so to speak, is the formula.

Being suitably placed for studying the object that you wish to commit to memory, draw its forms in your head, and to concentrate your attention the better, follow the forms, at a distance, with the end of your finger or anything pointed. Then shut your eyes, or look away from the object, and draw it again in the air.

These imaginary drawings, being naturally of the easiest possible execution, may be repeated very rapidly, and as often as you think necessary to help you to implant securely in your mind's eye the image of the thing of which you mean to make an actual drawing.

The manner in which this method is employed should depend upon the power of the student's memory. The abler ones may begin with the big lines of the mass, that is, the simplified impression of the whole effect, before attending to details. The weaker ones, being unable to grasp the whole subject at once, will have to make imaginary drawings of one part only over and over again, and stroke by stroke, in order that the impression may be, so to speak, encrusted on their mind. They will have to deal similarly with each part in turn, and when they finally come to the study of the subject as a whole, must repeat it over and over again in the same manner.

Again, if they cannot grasp both form and color at once, they should begin by making an abstract of the shadows.

Subject to slight modifications, all these prescriptions apply equally well to the studying of color by memory. In that case, imagine your finger to be a paint brush, and to better fix the attention, pass it over the subject, from a distance, as if you were actually painting the various tints. Then turn your eyes away and repeat this imaginary painting in the air until the colored image of it appears so distinctly in your mind that you can reproduce it from memory in real paint.

These operations, which may perhaps appear at first sight odd and almost fantastic, have been proved to be very simple in practice, and offer advantages very readily appreciated.

In the execution of such drawings and paintings in our heads, our ideas and feelings are unhampered by material difficulties and have free play to follow their natural inclination. They need not be slavishly bound by the exact appearances of things, which they may modify at pleasure by selection, by abstraction, by adding to them or taking away from them, by emphasis or embellishment, in short, by grafting, as it were, the ideal upon the real.

Is not that truly an act of assimilation, whereby an artist, once he has made nature his own, is able, so to speak, to infuse her with his own personal sentiment?

Thus the procedure that I advocate must be admitted to exercise and cultivate simultaneously artistic memory, artistic intelligence, and artistic feeling. It is equally well adapted for advanced as for elementary study. Besides tending to develop the memory and the higher faculties, it will lead to the early formation of the excellent habit, only too rare, of devoting a few moments of head work to considering the model, before the hand work is allowed to begin.

Excerpted from *The Training of the Memory in Art and the Education of the Artist*, by Horace Lecoq De Boisbaudran, Macmillan And Co., London., ©1911, Pages 42-44.

Appendix II
• Harold Speed: The Visual Memory •

Harold Speed's book, *The Practice and Science of Drawing*, written in 1913, is still considered the standard work on the subject of learning to draw. His chapter on the visual memory is presented here. I have left his spellings intact.

The memory is the great storehouse of artistic material, the treasures of which the artist may know little about until a chance association lights up some of its dark recesses. From early years the mind of the young artist has been storing up impressions in these mysterious chambers, collected from nature's aspects, works of art, and anything that comes within the field of vision. It is from this store that the imagination draws its material, however fantastic and remote from natural appearances the forms it may assume.

How much our memory of pictures colours the impressions of nature we receive is probably not suspected by us, but who could say how a scene would appear to him, had he never looked at a picture? So sensitive is the vision to the influence of memory that, after seeing the pictures of some painter whose work has deeply impressed us, we are apt, while the memory of it is still fresh in our minds, to see things as he would paint them. On different occasions after leaving the National Gallery I can remember having seen Trafalgar Square as Paolo Veronese, Turner, or whatever painter may have impressed me in the Gallery, would have painted it, the memory of their work colouring the impression the scene produced.

But, putting aside the memory of pictures, let us consider the place of direct visual memory from nature in our work, pictures being indirect or second-hand impressions.

We have seen in an earlier chapter how certain painters in the nineteenth century, feeling how very second-hand and far removed from nature painting had become, started a movement to discard studio traditions and study nature with a single eye, taking their pictures out of doors, and endeavouring to wrest nature's secrets from her on the spot. The Pre-Raphaelite movement in England and the Impressionist movement in France were the results of this impulse. And it is interesting, by the way, to contrast the different manner in which this desire for more truth to nature affected the French and English temperaments. The intense individualism of the English sought out every detail, every leaf and flower for itself, painting them with a passion and intensity that made their painting a vivid medium for the expression of poetic ideas; while the more synthetic mind of the Frenchman approached this search for visual truth from the opposite point of view of the whole effect, finding in the large, generalised impression a new world of beauty. And his more logical mind led him to inquire into the nature of light, and so to invent a technique founded on scientific principles.

But now the first blush of freshness has worn off the new movement, painters have begun to see that if anything but very ordinary effects are to be attempted, this painting on the spot must give place to more reliance on the memory.

Memory has this great advantage over direct vision: it retains more vividly the essential things, and has a habit of losing what is unessential to the pictorial impression.

But what is the essential in a painting? What is it that makes one want to paint at all? Ah! Here we approach very debatable and shadowy ground, and we can do little but ask questions, the answer to which will vary with each individual temperament. What is it that these rays of light striking our retina convey to our brain, and from our brain to whatever is ourselves, in the seat of consciousness above this? What is this mysterious correspondence set up between something within and something without, that at times sends such a clamour of harmony through our whole being? Why do certain combinations of sound in music and of form and colour in art affect us so profoundly? What are the laws governing harmony in the universe, and whence do they come? It is hardly trees and sky, earth, or flesh and blood, as such, that interest the artist; but rather that through these things in memorable moments he is permitted a consciousness of deeper things, and impelled to seek utterance for what is moving him. It is the record of these rare moments in which one apprehends truth in things seen that the artist wishes to convey to others. But these moments, these flashes of inspiration which are at the inception of every vital picture, occur but seldom. What the painter has to do is to fix them vividly in his memory, to snapshot them, as it were, so that they may stand by him during the toilsome procedure of the painting, and guide the work.

This initial inspiration, this initial flash in the mind, need not be the result of a scene in nature, but may of course be purely the work of the imagination; a composition, the sense of which flashes across the mind. But in either case the difficulty is to preserve vividly the sensation of this original artistic impulse. And in the case of its having been derived from nature direct, as is so often the case in modern art, the system of painting continually on the spot is apt to lose touch with it very soon. For in the continual observation of anything you have set your easel before day after day, comes a series of impressions, more and more commonplace, as the eye becomes more and more familiar with the details of the subject. And ere long the original emotion that was the reason of the whole work is lost sight of, and one of those pictures or drawings giving a catalogue of tired objects more or less ingeniously arranged (that we all know so well) is the result—work utterly lacking in the freshness and charm of true inspiration. For however commonplace the subject seen by the artist in one of his "flashes," it is clothed in a newness and surprise that charm us, be it only an orange on a plate.

Now a picture is a thing of paint upon a flat surface, and a drawing is a matter of certain marks upon a paper, and how to translate the intricacies of a visual or imagined impression to the prosaic terms of masses of coloured pigment or lines and tones is the business with which our technique is concerned. The ease, therefore, with which a painter will be able to remember an impression in a form from which he can work, will depend upon his power to analyse vision in this technical sense. The more one knows about what may be called the anatomy of picture-making—how certain forms produce certain effects, certain colours or arrangements other effects, &c.—the easier will it be for him to carry away a visual memory of his subject that will stand by him during the long hours of his labours at the picture. The more he knows of the expressive powers of lines and tones, the more easily will he be able to observe the vital things in nature that convey the impression he wishes to memorise.

It is not enough to drink in and remember the emotional side of the matter, although this must be done fully, but if a memory of the subject is to be carried away that will be of service technically, the scene must be committed to memory in terms of whatever medium you intend to employ for reproducing it—in the case of a drawing, lines and tones. And the impression will have to be analysed into these terms as if you were actually drawing the scene on some imagined piece of paper in your mind. The faculty of doing this is not to be acquired all at once, but it is amazing of how much development it is capable. Just as the faculty of committing to memory long poems or plays can be developed, so can the faculty of remembering visual things. This subject has received little attention in art schools until just recently. But it is not yet so systematically done as it might be. Monsieur Lecoq de Boisbaudran in France experimented with pupils in this memory training, beginning with very simple things like the outline of a nose, and going on to more complex subjects by easy stages, with the most surprising results. And there is no doubt that a great deal more can and should be done in this direction than is at present attempted. What students should do is to form a habit of making every day in their sketch-book a drawing of something they have seen that has interested them, and that they have made some attempt at memorising. Don't be discouraged if the results are poor and disappointing at first—you will find that by persevering your power of memory will develop and be of the greatest service to you in your after work. Try particularly to remember the spirit of the subject, and in this memory-drawing some scribbling and fumbling will necessarily have to be done. You cannot expect to be able to draw definitely and clearly from memory, at least at first, although your aim should always be to draw as frankly and clearly as you can.

Let us assume that you have found a subject that moves you and that, being too fleeting to draw on the spot, you wish to commit to memory. Drink a full enjoyment of it, let it soak in, for the recollection of this will be of the utmost use to you afterwards in guiding your memory-drawing. This mental impression is not difficult to recall; it is the visual impression in terms of line and tone that is difficult to remember. Having experienced your full enjoyment of the artistic matter in the subject, you must next consider it from the material side, as a flat, visual impression, as this is the only form in which it can be expressed on a flat sheet of paper. Note the proportions of the main lines, their shapes and disposition, as if you were drawing it, in fact do the whole drawing in your mind, memorising the forms and proportions of the different parts, and fix it in your memory to the smallest detail.

If only the emotional side of the matter has been remembered, when you come to draw it you will be hopelessly at sea, as it is remarkable how little the memory retains of the appearance of things constantly seen, if no attempt has been made to memorise their visual appearance.

The true artist, even when working from nature, works from memory very largely. That is to say, he works to a scheme in tune to some emotional enthusiasm with which the subject has inspired him in the first instance. Nature is always changing, but he does not change the intention of his picture. He always keeps before him the initial impression he sets out to paint, and only selects from nature those things that play up to it. He is a feeble artist, who copies individually the parts of a scene with whatever effect they may have at the moment he is doing them, and then expects the sum total to make a picture. If circumstances permit, it is always as well to make in the first instance a rapid sketch that shall, whatever it may lack, at least contain the main disposition of the masses and lines of your composition seen under the influence of the enthusiasm that has inspired the work. This will be of great value afterwards in freshening your memory when in the labour of the work the original impulse gets dulled. It is seldom that the vitality of this first sketch is surpassed by the completed work, and often, alas! it is far from equalled.

In portrait painting and drawing the memory must be used also. A sitter varies very much in the impression he gives on different days, and the artist must in the early sittings, when his mind is fresh, select the aspect he means to paint and afterwards work largely to the memory of this.

Always work to a scheme on which you have decided, and do not flounder on in the hope of something turning up as you go along. Your faculties are never so active and prone to see something interesting and fine as when the subject is first presented to them. This is the time to decide your scheme; this is the time to take your fill of the impression you mean to convey. This is the time to learn your subject thoroughly and decide on what you wish the picture to be. And having decided this, work straight on, using nature to support your original impression, but don't be led off by a fresh scheme because others strike you as you go along. New schemes will do so, of course, and every new one has a knack of looking better than your original one. But it is not often that this is so; the fact that they are new makes them appear to greater advantage than the original scheme to which you have got accustomed. So that it is not only in working away from nature that the memory is of use, but actually when working directly in front of nature.

To sum up, there are two aspects of a subject, the one luxuriating in the sensuous pleasure of it, with all of spiritual significance it may consciously or unconsciously convey, and the other concerned with the lines, tones, shapes, &c., and their rhythmic ordering, by means of which it is to be expressed—the matter and manner, as they may be called.

And, if the artist's memory is to be of use to him in his work, both these aspects must be memorised, and of the two the second will need the most attention. But although there are these two aspects of the subject, and each must receive separate attention when memorising it, they are in reality only two aspects of the same thing, which in the act of painting or drawing must be united if a work of art is to result. When a subject first flashes upon an artist he delights in it as a painted or drawn thing, and feels instinctively the treatment it will require. In good draughtsmanship the thing felt will guide and govern everything, every touch will be instinct with the thrill of that first impression. The craftsman mind, so laboriously built up, should by now have become an instinct, a second nature, at the direction of a higher consciousness. At such times the right strokes, the right tones come naturally and go on the right place, the artist being only conscious of a fierce joy and a feeling that things are in tune and going well for once. It is the thirst for this glorious enthusiasm, this fusing of matter and manner, this act of giving the spirit within outward form, that spurs the artist on at all times, and it is this that is the wonderful thing about art.

Excerpted from, *The Practice and Science of Drawing*, by Harold Speed, Seeley, Service & Co. Limited, London., ©1913, Pages 256-264.

Appendix III
•Curves or Facets?•

Whether to begin a drawing via curves or facets is a contentious subject. Nonetheless, it is an important one to understand when memory training because how you perceive the main shapes of your sources will, in part, be predetermined by whether you prefer to curve or facet.

Harold Speed, in his book, *The Practice and Science of Drawing*, suggests that observational drawings should begin with a flattening of the curves as a means to grab the essential aspects of the whole of the object. Others disagree.

R. H. Ives Gammell, who taught two of my teachers, writes about the uncertain role the curve-flattening approach to drawing has in an artist's training. One of Gammell's first teachers was William Sergeant Kendall, on whose approach he comments on here:

> *A feeling for underlying flat planes undeniably gives character to the expression of form. It has appealed to some painters more than others. Among the great masters, Hals carried the principle farthest while Ingres leaned the most in the opposite direction. Pushed to the extreme of absurdity, it became the basic justification of Cubism. But it is at least doubtful whether beginners should be subjected to this kind of discipline. After a lifetime of painting, I find myself still uncertain whether such training at an early stage is valuable or whether it is positively harmful to the pupil.[1]*

Gammell then goes on to quote Boisbaudran:

> *Breaking up all forms of nature, including those of the human figure, into squares, angles and triangles, cannot fail to affect the child's notion of real form; for children are highly impressionable. By thus destroying all grace, suppleness, and delicacy, and forcing on their young attention shapeless masses, exaggerated into squares and angles, the delicate growth of a true feeling for beauty and harmony is destroyed in the bud.[2]*

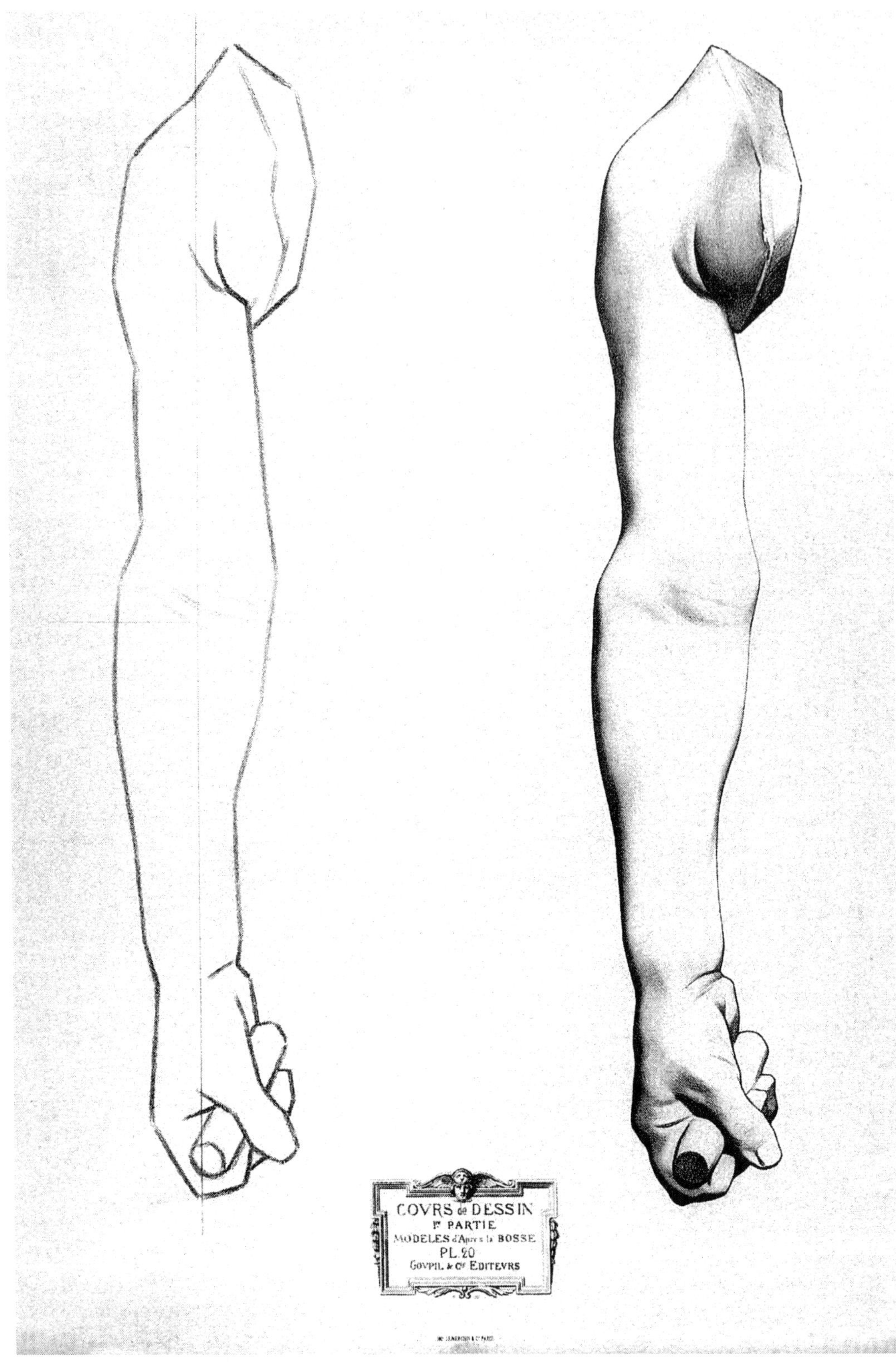

A plate from the *Bargue-Gérôme Drawing Course* (*Cours de Dessin*),
from the 1860s, showing the faceting approach to outline.

Gammell concludes:

> *But all this is an open question and a certain amount of schooling in simplifying complex forms into flat planes has much to be said for it. I am grateful to Kendall for his emphasis on it. In later years Paxton[3] criticized the system adversely. DeCamp,[4] on the other hand, advocated it as his own painting shows. He considered Paxton's drawing, which he admired, overstressed the curves. Paxton told me that DeCamp's work, which he admired, was slightly flawed by his over-emphasis of the flat planes. And so the reader of these notes who is seeking to reconstruct a sound method of teaching drawing will have to decide this matter for himself.[5]*

Although Boisbaudran directly refutes the faceting approach to drawing, he also contradicts himself in Appendix I of his book:

> *In calculating a shape, one may imagine it inscribed in a simple elementary figure, such as a square, a circle, a triangle, etc., and decide how far it approaches or recedes from the imaginary figure described about it.*

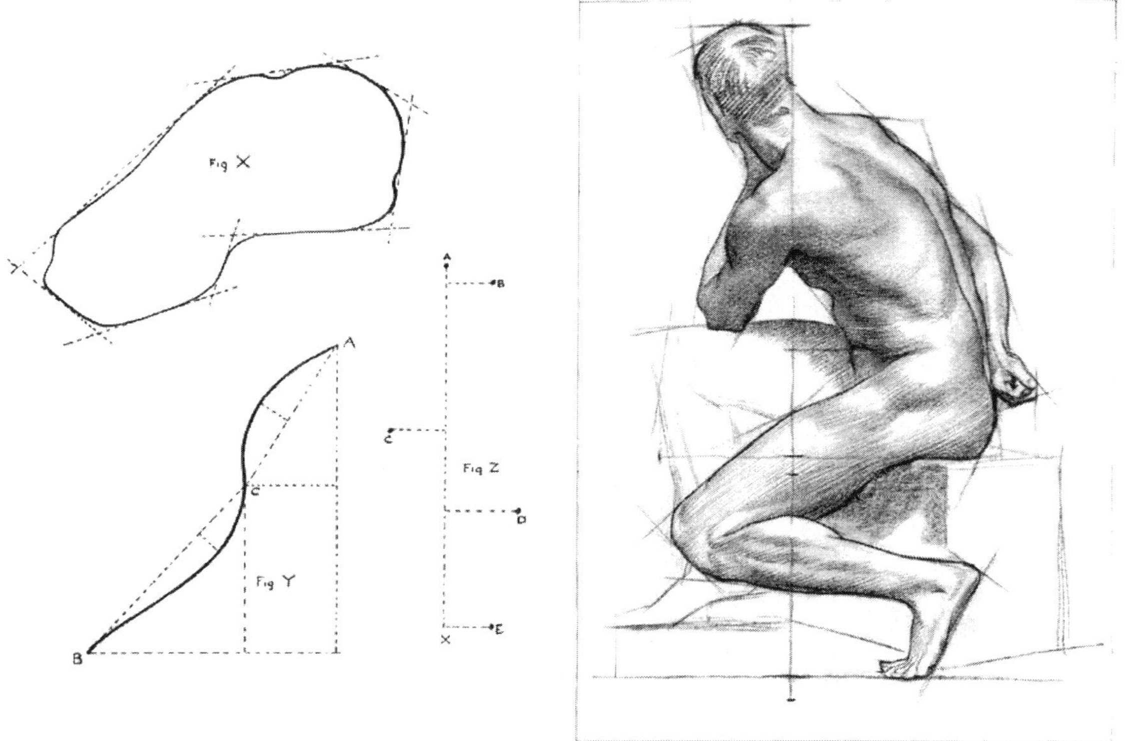

Plates from Harold Speed's book, *The Practise and Science of Drawing*, from 1913, showing faceting (left) and building up a drawing (right).

In a 1912 Burlington Magazine review of Boisbaudran's book, the reviewer comments on Boisbaudran's initial criticism of the faceting approach.

Doubtless this method has produced awful work from bad students, but detail, unless you trace it mechanically, is almost impossible to get right unless you have first a general geometrical skeleton into which to fit it. In fact no master or student could give detail its correct and proper place without having either on the paper or in his head some system of angles and masses for the whole.[6]

Alas, we are left with but one conclusion, that both approaches have their adherents as well as their varying degrees of success. Those who follow the faceting approach would be wise to remember that nature contains very few straight lines. Do not let the self-imposed flats blind you to the observed facts. Likewise, those who dislike faceting but prefer curves should be mindful of the relationships between the curves. Accurately representing a curved form depends not only upon the correctness of the curve but also on the relationship that the curve has to the surrounding forms.

The main content of this appendix comes from a post on my blog. I have revised it for this book: http://www.studiorousar.com/2011/01/09/squaring-the-circle/

1 R. H. Ives Gammell from his unpublished autobiography©1981, 1995 Elizabeth Ives Hunter.
2 Boisbaudran, Horace Lecoq de. *The Training of the Memory in Art and the Education of the Artist*. London: Macmillan and Co. Limited, 1914. Page 61.
3 William MacGregor Paxton was Gammell's final teacher.
4 Joseph DeCamp advised Gammell when Gammell was a young man and searching for a teacher.
5 R. H. Ives Gammell from his unpublished autobiography ©1981, 1995 Elizabeth Ives Hunter.
6 From a review of *The Training of the Memory in Art and the Education of the Artist* by Lecoq de Boisbaudran, *The Burlington Magazine for Connoisseurs*, Vol. 21, No. 113 (Aug., 1912), Page 300.

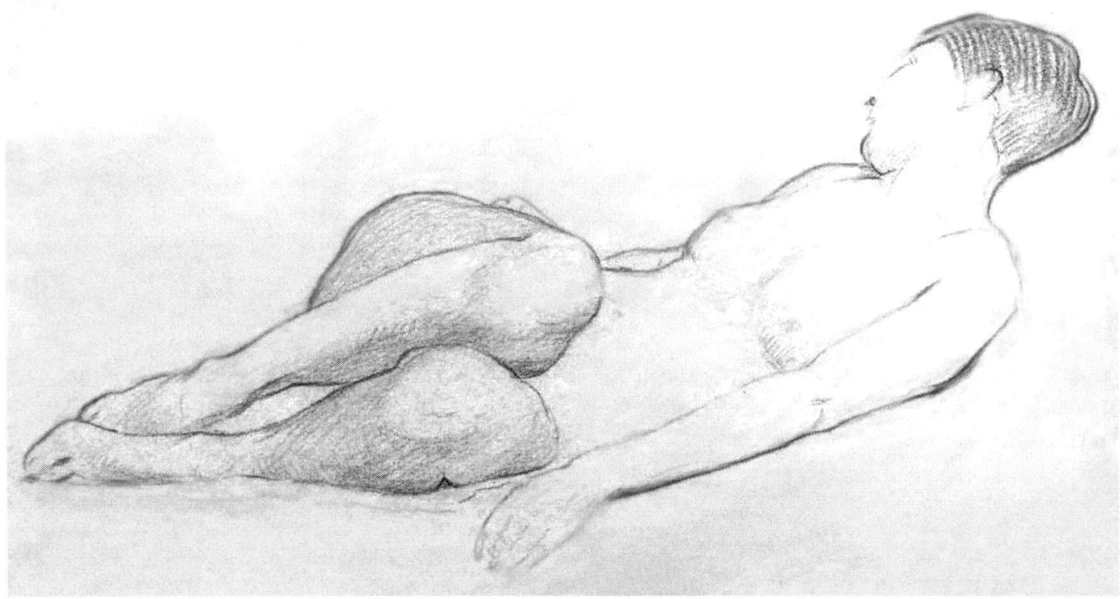

Nude Study (1929) -by William McGregor Paxton

Appendix IV
• Copying Old Master Drawings •

The invaluable training derived from making exact copies of fine drawings has been recognized by great draftsmen from Leonardo to Degas and the practice was recommended to me later by Philip Hale and Paxton.[1] -R. H. Ives Gammell

Although tangential to the subject of memory drawing, copy work is an important aspect to many students' training. Exactly how does one go about doing that? First and foremost, it must be recognized that when copying another's drawing or painting, the goal is to try to get inside the master's head. This is done in order to learn to see nature as they saw it. Your feelings or impressions are largely irrelevant to this process, and if that is not recognized at the outset, the exercise will be of little use. It is true that the Old Masters sometimes freely copied other Old Masters. Rubens' copy of Caravaggio's *Entombment* is perhaps the most famous example, but these were mainly done as memory aides or attempts at recomposing the scene. Their goal was not training.

When choosing an Old Master drawing to copy, the main thing to look for is whether or not the drawing is highly accomplished. While it may generally be true that drawings from lesser masters have qualities which are admirable, it is always better to learn from the top. Master drawings are deemed masterful because of many characteristics and when

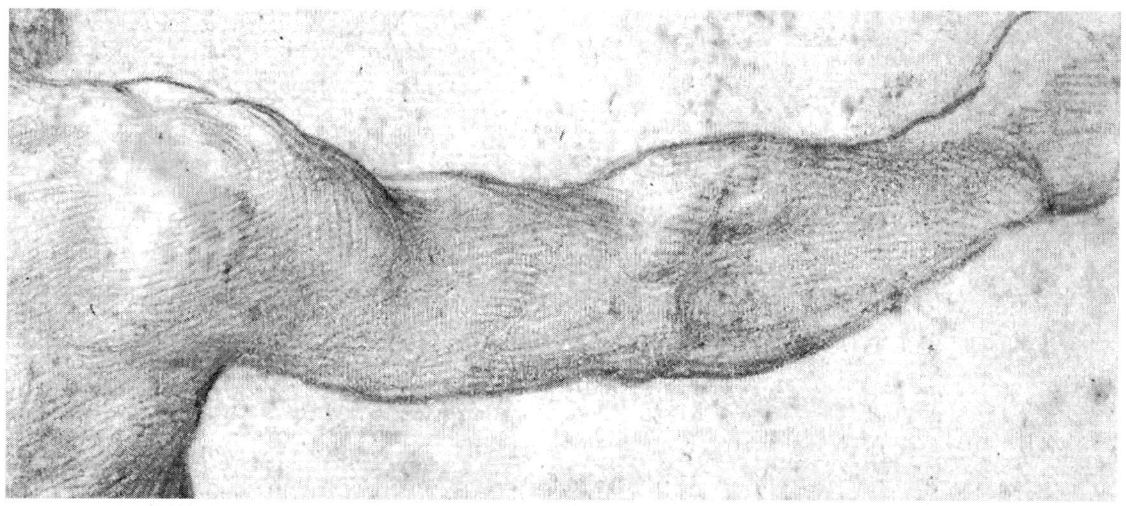

A Study of Two Male Nudes (detail) -by Raphael

copying these kinds of drawings you will naturally learn them. The same is true for copying drawings which are not as accomplished; you will likely pick up bad habits.

Copying drawings which are obviously thumbnail sketches may not be a good idea either. If your goal is to learn how an Old Master simplified their observations into a quick sketch, that is fine. However, if your goal is to learn how to represent form in a linear fashion, it is best to use a finished drawing as your source.

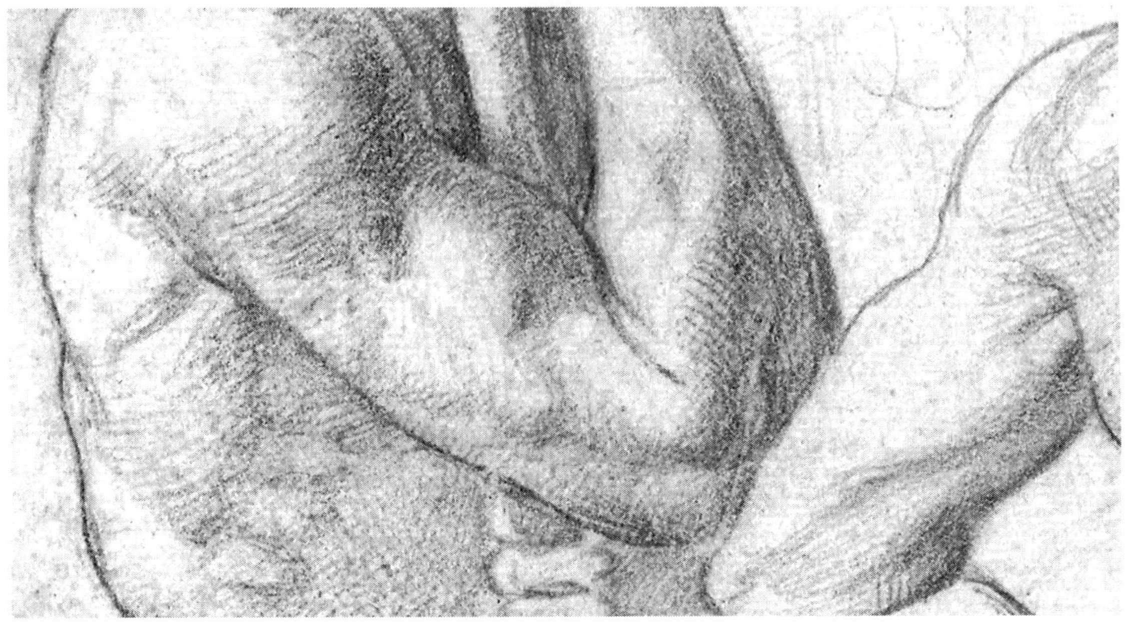

A Study of Two Male Nudes (detail) -by Raphael

For centuries, students have copied Raphael's drawings, and today his drawings are still excellent choices. Ingres, himself an admirer of Raphael, also did drawings that are worthy of study. For those who are more interested in charcoal, Rubens and Watteau are fine choices.

In my opinion, many of Michelangelo's drawings are a bit problematic for a student copyist. As beautiful as they are, they often contain exaggerated anatomy and in some cases, proportions. The student should remember that Michelangelo did his drawings for the purposes of his own study, and as preparatory work for his paintings and sculpture. They were not meant to be artworks in and of themselves. I do not prohibit my students from copying his drawings. However, I merely suggest a cautionary approach.

Your source does not have to be the actual size of the original drawing although it might help. Inevitably the question of sight-size is mentioned. Copying can of course be done using sight-size, literal measuring or simply by eye, and one can stand or sit. The exactness Gammell talks about is what will get you into the mind of Raphael, and if you can manage that exactly, by doing the copy comparatively, then so be it. Just know that if you draw much smaller than your source, you will miss some of the nuances in it. Draw too large and you may be forced to make things up that are not actually present.

Besides the obvious shape and value aspects, the other areas of importance regarding exactness are line variation and shading quality. In the detail images, notice how the lines of the contours are somewhat ribbon-like, meaning that they are variously light and dark, thick and thin. Part of the copyist's job is to discern why the lines are drawn the way that they are. Continually ask yourself these questions and others like them. Are they thick or thin when that part of the body represents bone, muscle or fat? Are they lighter or darker when crossing at those areas? Think about the representation of depth or form. Do the thick/thin and light/dark lines have parts to play in representing that?

How about the halftones and shadows? Are the shadows drawn in as angled, parallel lines like Harold Speed recommends in his book, or do they follow the form? How about the halftone lines? Do they crisscross each other or are they more singularly distinct?

Are the strokes sure, or does it seem like Raphael is searching out his way in sketchy lines? Was he drawing both sides of the body or a limb at the same time, or simply going around the contour?

Which paper to use is a concern, but from a learning standpoint it is possibly less of an issue than the medium. However, the correct value of paper can have a significant effect on copy work. The paper Raphael used for the drawing presented here has some weave, enough to slightly affect his ability to smoothly lay down a solid tone. Then again, there are few large areas of smooth tone as this is a linear drawing. I will not recommend a brand of paper though, just make sure that it is not student-grade or too rough.

Your next concern is medium. The Old Masters did not have #2 yellow pencils. They used a variety of materials, many of which had to be made or modified by themselves. Sanguine is a good example of this. That which is commonly available in art stores nowadays is usually in squared stick form and is often full of wax (which is used as a binder). Of course good art might be created with this, but you'll likely end up fighting the material when doing a copy.

The Raphael drawing highlighted in this appendix was done in natural sanguine, which is a form of a red chalk. I was taught to break shards off of the natural chunks to achieve a point, but Matthew Collins has a great post about creating your own sanguine which will give you far more control: http://matthewjamescollins.com/2010/08/11/sanguine-drawing/

This is not to say that you will fail if you use something else. Pencil or even sharply pointed charcoal may work well. It depends upon the drawing. A linear example, like this Raphael, demands a linear copy and therefore a linear medium, or at least one that is treated in that way. One could even use a quality brick-red pencil. The larger point is that the medium affects the result.

At a minimum it is helpful to lightly place marks where the top and bottom of the image will go and also to draw a center or plumb line. It is clear that Raphael did not block-in this drawing, like I and others teach when doing a cast drawing. You may, of course, do the copy that way, just make it very light and be aware that the block-in is simply a set of guides. If you prefer, begin by lightly drawing the shapes you see, attempting to achieve all of the grace and relationships from the start. That is likely how Raphael did the drawing.

Of immense help will be doing your own life drawing concurrent with the copy. Your drawing does not have to be in the pose of the drawing being copied though because learning how an Old Master represented natural forms is not tied to those forms. It is ultimately a set of principles that you are learning via the copy. After you do enough of them, along with looking at and doing a lot of drawings, these principles will become second nature. Putting into practice what you learn, while you are learning it, is a sure way to make it a part of you. You will stop consciously analyzing what you are looking at and just begin to do it naturally. You will see the object drawn, before you actually draw it.

Finally, remember that line drawing is a construct or a convention. It is a made up representation of the source object because there are no natural lines in nature (other than things like strands of hair). Therefore, the artist has to develop a way of using line to represent non-line. Immerse yourself in Raphael, Rubens, Ingres, Degas and Watteau drawings, among others, and learn how each used line to delineate form.

Make copies, young man, many copies.
You can only become a good artist by copying the masters.
-Ingres

The main content of this appendix comes from a post on my blog. I have revised it for this book: http://www.studiorousar.com/2012/04/18/copying-old-master-drawings/

1 R. H. Ives Gammell from his unpublished autobiography. ©1981, 1995 by Elizabeth Ives Hunter.

·Glossary·

Word definitions can be fluid, especially when it comes to art terms. Art movements, schools and ateliers sometimes end up defining their own terms or redefining the ones already being used to better suit their purposes. Translations between languages can also alter a word's historical, or traditional definition. Some of the words which follow are scientific terms. I have slightly altered their definitions to fit the subject of this book.

Most of the definitions for the art terms were the ones that I was taught. Others resulted from conclusions drawn from my own research. A radio talk show host named Dennis Prager likes to tell his audience that he prefers clarity over agreement. It is in that spirit that I present the following definitions.

The reader should note that not all of the words in this glossary will be found in this book. However, further research on the various topics presented here may turn up connections which require a common understanding.

Atelier

Atelier means "workshop" in French and in the nineteenth century it described small art studio-schools run by master artists who taught painting. Pronounced "atel-yay".

In 1971 Richard Lack founded *Atelier Lack* in Minneapolis, Minnesota. Lack is credited with popularizing the *atelier* movement (as well as sight-size) in the US. Currently the term is used by many art schools whether or not they have any connection with Lack or his teacher R. H. Ives Gammell.

Afterimage

The word *afterimage* has two definitions. Pertaining to memory drawing, it is an optical illusion which for a brief period of time after staring at the source, allows you to continue to *see* the image on your retina.

Bed-bug line
The boundary between light and shade. Also called, the *terminator* or the *shadow line*.

Big look
Seeing whatever is being drawn or painted as a whole, unified image. Each part of what is seen is compared with every other part as well as the whole. Cognitive psychologists term this kind of seeing, *holistic*.

Bottom-up processing
Perception using *bottom-up processing* does not rely upon a mental understanding of what the object actually is (e.g., an apple, a chair, etc.). Rather, it is concerned with the visual properties of the object independent of the object's classification. This is drawing what you see, not what you know. See *top-down processing*.

Chunking
The process of grouping discrete pieces of information. This process helps a person to recall more pieces of information than would otherwise be possible. Phone numbers, for example, are chunked.

Classical Realism
Coined by Richard Lack in 1982 when he was asked by a museum director to differentiate the style of representational painting practiced by the heirs of the Boston tradition from other representational artists who were active during that time. At present the definition of the term has become clouded. To the general public virtually any contemporary realist painting is considered to be within the realm of *Classical Realism*.

Cognitive psychology
Cognitive psychology is a branch of psychology which studies how our mind perceives.

Construction
Drawing via *construction* can mean a number of things, such as using ovoids, block forms, anatomy or gesture lines.

Cool
Along with *warm*, *cool* is a relative term which describes how one color appears in relation to another. Despite their non-specific nature, *cool* and *warm* are very important terms for artists engaged in naturalistic seeing and they have a long history of use. See *warm*.

Dual-coding
Combining relevant verbal observations or descriptions about an object or scene with visual observations. This helps our brain to store those observations in long-term memory. It also enhances our ability to recall them.

Faceting

Faceting means beginning a drawing (or painting) with a flattening of the curves as a means to grab the essential aspects of the whole of the object.

Gestalt

Gestalt is a German word that is difficult to define in English. For our purposes it basically means *form* or *shape* and in the context of this book it is further defined as *a unified whole*. See also *big look*.

Holistic seeing

See *big look*.

Long-term memory

A memory which is stored and then recalled after a period of time is a *long-term memory*. One goal of memory drawing exercises is to improve the capabilities of your visual long-term memory.

Naturalistic seeing

A combination of the *big look* and a *persistent focus*. Seeing in this way is based upon the relationships between one shape, value, edge or color and another. Also called *unity of effect* or *impressionistic seeing*.

Observe, observation

See *visual perception*.

Perceive, perception

See *visual perception*.

Persistent focus

Persistent focus is focusing on one area of the scene while perceiving areas of the scene which are away from your focal point but within your peripheral vision.

Piecemeal seeing

The opposite of the *big look*. This type of seeing considers everything by itself, unrelated to the whole of the image.

Rehearsal

One process for moving *short-term* and *working* memories into *long-term memory* is rehearsal. In the visual realm this means thinking about the visual aspects of the object or scene when not actually observing them.

Sight-size

Sight-size is an approach to drawing or painting while viewing the model and the artwork simultaneously from a selected position so that both images appear the same size to the artist. This setup allows the artist to directly compare nature with the artwork and to more easily see and record the impression of the whole of the scene.

Short-term memory

A memory which lasts only a few seconds and requires no further mental manipulation is short-term. To test yours, see here: http://faculty.washington.edu/chudler/stm0.html

Top-down processing

Top-down processing, relative to drawing, is perception which begins with an learned idea, a preconceived view or an association. The idea can be based upon many things: construction, form, concept, anatomy or any combination of them. This is drawing from one's knowledge, as opposed to the observed image itself, by presupposing principles onto the perception of the image. See *bottom-up processing*.

Visual perception

Visual perception has at least two components:
1. Detection, which is your mind fixating on something your eye sees.
2. Recognition, which is your mind's awareness of what the object or scene is.

Warm

A relative term which describes how one color appears in relation to another. See *cool*.

Working memory

A memory which is further manipulated but not stored long term is called a working-memory. When you switch your attention from the model to the drawing paper you are using your *working memory* to draw what you observed. The act of drawing those observations can help move the working memory into your *long-term memory*.

·Index·

A

abstract shapes 35, 50, 101
afterimage 40, 50
analysis 37, 43, 44, 45, 50, 55, 59, 63, 76, 77, 86,
 87, 101
Aristotle 22, 30, 35, 37, 39, 71

B

big look 21, 35, 55, 83, 87, 106
Boisbaudran, Horace Lecoq de 11, 13, 14, 19, 20,
 21, 22, 23, 24, 25, 26, 27, 30, 83, 91, 111,
 113, 117, 121, 123, 124
bottom-up processing 34. See also *top-down
 processing*

C

Catterson-Smith, Robert 27, 30
Cavé , Marie Elisabeth Blavot Boulanger 19, 25,
 26, 31
Cavé Method 25, 26, 31
Cecil, Charles H. 11, 134, 136
Collins, Matthew J. 5, 104, 108
Corot, Jean-Baptiste-Camille 15, 30
Crane, Bruce 17, 30
Crane, Walter 15, 30
curves and facets 7, 13, 121, 123

D

DeCamp, Joseph Rodefer 124
Degas, Edgar 18, 19, 30, 87, 100, 103, 125, 127
Delacroix, Ferdinand Victor Eugène 19, 25, 26
Descartes, René 40
directly seeing 45. See also *bottom-up processing*
dual coding 37, 40

E

Eakins, Thomas 24, 30

F

Fantin-Latour, Henri 20, 24
focus 69

G

Gammell, R. H. Ives 11, 13, 14, 30, 92, 97, 121,
 123, 124, 125, 127
gamut 42, 72, 91, 94, 101, 102
Gérôme, Jean Léon 10, 24, 77, 87, 89, 122
gestalt 35, 36, 40 See also *big look*
gesture drawing 83, 84
Gleyre, Marc Gabriel Charles 24

H

Harrison, Birge 100
holistic seeing 35, 83. See also *big look* and *gestalt*
Hunt, William Morris 17, 18, 30

I

indirectly knowing 45. See also *bottom-up
 processing*
Inness, George 17, 30, 100

L

Lack, Richard F. 11, 14, 91, 99, 102
landscape painting 9, 13, 18, 101
Legros, Alphonse 20, 24
Leonardo da Vinci 9, 84
LeSueur, Annette 11
Lutz, E. G. 28, 29, 44, 135

M

maquettes 107, 108
memory and imagination 9, 15, 16, 19, 35, 99,
 102, 105, 115, 116

memory and perception 10, 12, 21, 22, 33, 34, 35, 36, 37, 38, 39, 40, 68, 71, 75, 83, 91, 93, 95, 96, 97, 106, 136
memory painting 9

O

Old Masters 16, 19, 25, 26, 125, 126

P

Paxton, William MacGregor 124
perceptual learning 34, 36, 91
photographic memory 33, 38, 39, 40
photography 9, 10, 39, 63, 102
Poore, Henry 84, 89
Practical Course in Memory Drawing 28, 29, 31

R

relationships 29, 35, 37, 46, 47, 71, 76, 93, 96, 101, 106
relative. See *relationships*
Reynolds, Sir Joshua 16, 23, 30

S

seeing
  analysis 55
seeing the whole. See *big look*
sight-impression 29, 30, 44, 59
Shepard & Metzler rotation task 106, 109
shut-eye drawing 27
Sight-size 92, 127, 134, 135, 136
Speed, Harold 7, 13, 115, 117, 119, 121, 123, 127

T

The Training of the Memory in Art and the Education of the Artist 14, 30, 111, 113, 124
top-down processing 34. See also *bottom-up processing*

V

vision
  inward vision 16, 30
  outward vision 15, 16

W

Whistler, James MacNeil 24, 31

A Brief Biography of the Author

Darren R. Rousar studied privately with Richard Lack and attended Atelier LeSueur (both in Minnesota) as well as Studio Cecil-Graves in Florence, Italy. During the mid-1990's he was the assistant director and an instructor at Charles Cecil Studios in Florence, after which he became vice president of The Minnesota River School of Fine Art in Burnsville, Minnesota.

He has been a professional artist and teacher for more than 20 years. His paintings are focused mainly on Christian themes. Darren is currently an art teacher and technology coordinator/coach at Providence Academy in Plymouth, Minnesota. In addition to authoring this book, he is the author of two books about sight-size, *Cast Drawing Using the Sight-Size Approach* and *Cast Painting Using the Sight-Size Approach* and the producer of a companion DVD, *Sight-Size and the Art of Seeing*. Through his company, Velatura Press, he republished an expanded edition of E. G. Lutz's 1921 book, *Drawing Made Easy*. In 2013, Velatura Press also republished *Landscape Painting*, a combined edition of Asher B. Durand's *Letters on Landscape Painting* with Birge Harrison's *Landscape Painting*.

For more information about Darren, his work and ongoing memory-drawing exercises, please see www.StudioRousar.com.

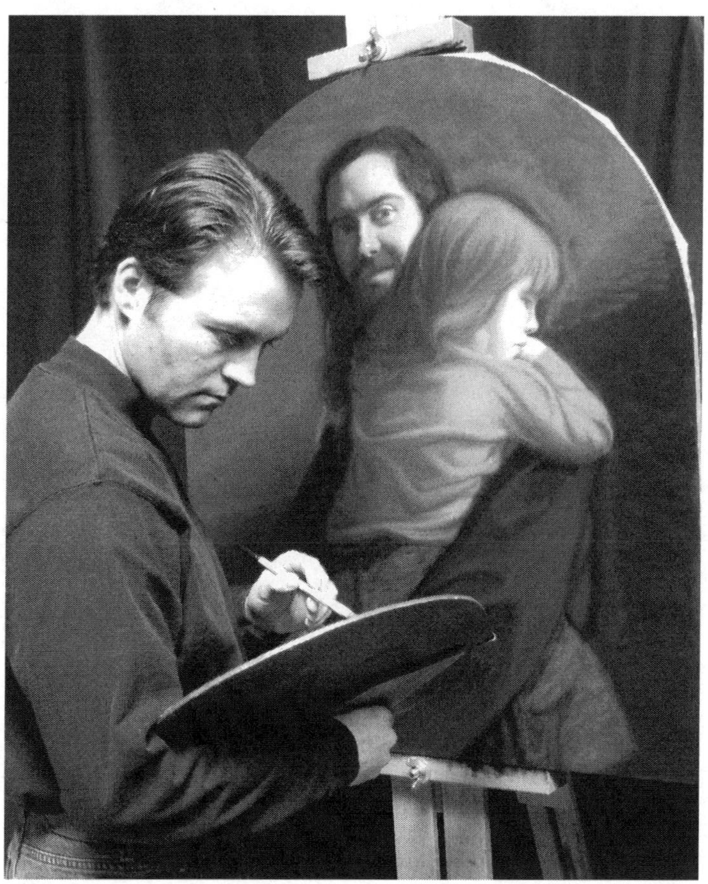

Sight-Size related books from other publishers

Painting the Visual Impression by Richard Whitney
Some have called *Painting the Visual Impression* "Crib Notes of Art" and "The Bible." Whatever one calls it, one thing is sure, this book is chock full of information every artist should know. Written by one of America's finest portrait and landscape artists, Richard Whitney's book should be read over and over again by the student and professional alike.
Painting the Visual Impression is published by Richard Whitney and available through his website at www.crescentpond.com/rwbooklet.html

Sculpting From Life - A Studio Manual of the Sight-Size Method by Jason Arkles
This is the first and only instructional manual written about the sight-size method as applied to sculpture. The blossoming atelier tradition in the United States and abroad has changed the way contemporary artists are trained, but scant attention had been paid to how figurative sculpture fits into this tradition until now. 157 pages and over 200 illustrations guide the reader through every aspect of figurative clay modelling, including bas-relief work, portraiture, and figure modeling, how to equip and outfit a studio, how to hire and use models, and more. The sight-size method is a strikingly different approach to clay sculpture than is offered by any other how-to manual. Combining optical principles and studio practice dating back five centuries and passed from master to apprentice right down to the author himself, the sight-size method is a philosophy of perception as much as a powerful tool for the sculptor. Written for teachers and students alike, *Sculpting from Life* is available through Amazon and other online booksellers.

Sight-Size Portraiture by Nicholas Beer
Nick Beer has been teaching and painting at the Charles H. Cecil Studios in Florence since 1992. In addition to being a comprehensive manual of instruction, *Sight-Size Portraiture* includes a history of the technique, a critique of three historical texts, and a chapter on "The Philosophy of Seeing." This book will be invaluable to anyone interested in the art of portraiture. *Sight-Size Portraiture* is available through Amazon and other online booksellers.

Made in the USA
Monee, IL
07 July 2026